MS-Office
one step at a time

ALSO AVAILABLE

<u>By both authors:</u>

BP294 A Concise Introduction to Microsoft Works
BP306 A Concise Introduction to Ami Pro 3
BP319 Making MS-DOS Work for You
BP327 DOS - One step at a time
BP336 A Concise User's Guide to Lotus 1-2-3 Release 3.4
BP337 A Concise User's Guide to Lotus 1-2-3 for Windows
BP338 A Concise Introduction to Word for Windows
BP339 A Concise Introd'n to WordPerfect 5.2 for Windows
BP341 MS-DOS 6 Explained
BP343 A Concise Introd'n to Microsoft Works for Windows
BP346 Programming in Visual Basic for Windows
BP351 WordPerfect 6 Explained
BP352 Excel 5 Explained
BP353 WordPerfect 6.0 for Windows Explained
BP354 Word 6 for Windows Explained
BP362 Access - One step at a time
BP372 CA-SuperCalc for Windows Explained
BP387 Windows - One step at a time
BP388 Why not personalise your PC
BP399 Windows 95 - One step at a time
BP400 Windows 95 Explained

<u>By Noel Kantaris:</u>

BP232 A Concise Introduction to MS-DOS
BP250 Programming in FORTRAN 77
BP258 Learning to Program in C
BP259 A Concise Introduction to UNIX
BP260 A Concise Introduction to OS/2
BP261 A Concise Introduction to Lotus 1-2-3
BP264 A Concise Advanced User's Guide to MS-DOS
BP274 A Concise Introduction to SuperCalc 5
BP284 Programming in QuickBASIC
BP314 A Concise Introduction to Quattro Pro 3.0
BP325 A Concise User's Guide to Windows 3.1
BP330 A Concise User's Guide to Lotus 1-2-3 Release 2.4

MS-Office
one step at a time

by

N. Kantaris
and
P.R.M. Oliver

BERNARD BABANI (publishing) LTD
THE GRAMPIANS
SHEPHERDS BUSH ROAD
LONDON W6 7NF
ENGLAND

PLEASE NOTE

Although every care has been taken with the production of this book to ensure that any projects, designs, modifications and/or programs, etc., contained herewith, operate in a correct and safe manner and also that any components specified are normally available in Great Britain, the Publishers and Author(s) do not accept responsibility in any way for the failure (including fault in design) of any project, design, modification or program to work correctly or to cause damage to any equipment that it may be connected to or used in conjunction with, or in respect of any other damage or injury that may be so caused, nor do the Publishers accept responsibility in any way for the failure to obtain specified components.

Notice is also given that if equipment that is still under warranty is modified in any way or used or connected with home-built equipment then that warranty may be void.

© 1995 BERNARD BABANI (publishing) LTD

First Published - December 1995

British Library Cataloguing in Publication Data:

Kantaris Noel
MS-Office one step at a time
I. Title II. Oliver, Phil
005.369

ISBN 0 85934 402 9

Printed and Bound in Great Britain by Cox & Wyman Ltd, Reading

ABOUT THIS BOOK

MS-Office - one step at a time has been written to help users to get to grips with the integrated components of this package, namely, the word processor *Word 6 for Windows*, the spreadsheet *Excel 5*, the presentation graphics *PowerPoint 4*, and, if you have *MS-Office Pro*, the database *Access 2*. No previous knowledge of these packages is assumed.

The book does not describe how to install and use Microsoft Windows, or how to set up your computer's hardware, although some aspects of the Windows environment, which you will need to know, are described. If you need to know more about these topics, then may we suggest that you select an appropriate level book for your needs from the 'Also Available' list - the books are graduated in complexity with the less demanding *One step at a time* series, followed by the *Concise Introduction* series, followed by the *Concise User's guide* series, to the more detailed *Explained* series. They are all published by BERNARD BABANI (publishing) Ltd.

The individual applications which make up Microsoft Office are designed to work together and have the same look and feel, which results in an easy learning curve. For example, the majority of menus, toolbar buttons, and dialogue boxes are the same in each application, which gives them a consistent interface, and makes it easier to share information between them.

Below we list some of the capabilities of this latest version of Microsoft Office:

- You can create a document in Microsoft Word, and then embed a chart or a worksheet from Excel in the Word document.

- You can create a link between Microsoft Word and the chart or worksheet in Excel so that when you change the data in Excel, the Word document is updated automatically.

- You can open a Microsoft Word document in PowerPoint, automatically creating a slide for each heading that has the Heading 1 style.
- You can insert an Excel worksheet in a PowerPoint slide so that you can display it during a presentation.
- You can mail merge a letter written in Microsoft Word with a contact list in the Access database.
- If you have Microsoft Mail, you can route a Word document, a PowerPoint presentation, or an Excel worksheet to a group of reviewers, then accept or reject their revisions.

As you can see, the various applications within Microsoft Office can either be used by themselves or made to share information. This book introduces each application by itself, with sufficient detail to get you working.

The book was written with the busy person in mind. It is not necessary to learn all there is to know about a subject, when reading a few selected pages can usually do the same thing quite adequately. With the help of this book, it is hoped that you will be able to come to terms with Microsoft Office and get the most out of your computer in terms of efficiency, productivity and enjoyment, and that you will be able to do it in the shortest, most effective and informative way.

If you would like to purchase a Companion Disc for this or any of the listed books by the same author(s), containing the file/program listings which appear in them, then fill in the form at the back of the book and send it to P.R.M. Oliver at the stipulated address.

ABOUT THE AUTHORS

Noel Kantaris graduated in Electrical Engineering at Bristol University and after spending three years in the Electronics Industry in London, took up a Tutorship in Physics at the University of Queensland. Research interests in Ionospheric Physics, led to the degrees of M.E. in Electronics and Ph.D. in Physics. On return to the UK, he took up a Post-Doctoral Research Fellowship in Radio Physics at the University of Leicester, and then in 1973 a lecturing position in Engineering at the Camborne School of Mines, Cornwall, (part of Exeter University), where since 1978 he has also assumed the responsibility for the Computing Department.

Phil Oliver graduated in Mining Engineering at Camborne School of Mines in 1967 and since then has specialised in most aspects of surface mining technology, with a particular emphasis on computer related techniques. He has worked in Guyana, Canada, several Middle Eastern countries, South Africa and the United Kingdom, on such diverse projects as: the planning and management of bauxite, iron, gold and coal mines; rock excavation contracting in the UK; international mining equipment sales and international mine consulting for a major mining house in South Africa. In 1988 he took up a lecturing position at Camborne School of Mines (part of Exeter University) in Surface Mining and Management.

ACKNOWLEDGEMENTS

We would like to thank colleagues at the Camborne School of Mines for the helpful tips and suggestions which assisted us in the writing of this book.

TRADEMARKS

Intel is a registered trademark of Intel Corporation.

LaserJet is a registered trademark of Hewlett-Packard Company.

Microsoft, MS-DOS, MS-Windows, MS-Office, MS-Word, MS-Excel. MS-PowerPoint, MS-Access, and **Visual Basic** are registered trademarks of Microsoft Corporation.

PostScript is a registered trademark of Adobe Systems Incorporated.

Any other brand and product names are trademarks, or registered trademarks, of their respective companies.

CONTENTS

1. **PACKAGE OVERVIEW** 1
   - Hardware and Software Requirements 2
   - Installing MS-Office 3
   - Starting the Program 7
     - MS-Office Program Icons 8
   - The Mouse Pointers 9
   - Manipulating Windows 10
     - Changing the Active Window 11
     - Moving Windows and Dialogue Boxes 11
     - Sizing a Window 11
     - Minimising and Maximising Windows 12
     - Closing a Window 13
   - The Menu Bar Options 13
     - Shortcut Menus 14
     - Dialogue Boxes 15

2. **THE WORD WORD PROCESSOR** 17
   - Starting the Program 17
   - Getting Familiar with Word 18
   - The Word Screen 19
     - The Formatting Bar 23
     - The Status Bar 24
   - Using Help in Word 25

3. **WORD DOCUMENT BASICS** 27
   - Entering Text 27
   - Moving Around a Document 28
   - Templates and Paragraph Styles 29
     - Changing Paragraph Styles 29
   - Document Screen Displays 30
   - Changing Default Options 32
     - Modifying Margins 32
     - Changing the Default Paper Size 33
     - Modifying the Paper Source 34
     - Modifying the Page Layout 34
     - Changing Other Default Options 35
   - Saving to a File 36
     - Closing a Document 38

4. EDITING WORD DOCUMENTS 39
    Selecting Text 40
    Copying Blocks of Text 42
    Moving Blocks of Text 43
    Deleting Blocks of Text 43
    The Undo Command 44
    Finding and Changing Text 44
    Page Breaks 47
    Using the Spell Checker 48
    Printing Documents 49

5. FORMATTING WORD DOCUMENTS 53
    Formatting Text 53
    Text Enhancements 56
        Paragraph Alignment 56
        Paragraph Spacing 57
        Indenting Text 58
        Inserting Bullets 62
    Formatting with Page Tabs 63
    Formatting with Styles 64
        Paragraph Styles 65
        Document Templates 67

6. THE EXCEL SPREADSHEET 69
    Starting the Excel Program 69
    The Excel Screen 70
    Getting Familiar with Excel 72
    Using Help in Excel 73
    Worksheet Navigation 74
        Moving Between Sheets 76
        Rearranging Sheet Order 77
        Grouping Worksheets 77
        Shortcut Menus 77
    Viewing Multiple Work 78

7. FILLING IN A WORKSHEET 79
    Entering Information 79
        Selecting a Range of Cells 80
        Changing Text Alignment and Fonts 82

Saving a Worksheet 83
Opening a Worksheet 85
Formatting Entries 86
   Filling a Range by Example 86
   Entering Text, Numbers and Formulae 87
Using Functions 88
   Using the AutoSum Icon 89
Printing a Worksheet 91

8. ADVANCED SPREADSHEETS 93

Enhancing a Worksheet 93
   Header and Footer Icons and Codes 94
   Setting a Print Area 95
3-Dimensional Worksheets 97
   Manipulating Ranges 97
Copying Sheets into a Workbook 98
Linking Sheets 100
Relative and Absolute Cell Addresses 101
Freezing Panes on Screen 102

9. SPREADSHEET CHARTS 103

Preparing for a Column Chart 103
The ChartWizard 105
   Saving and Naming Charts 111
Pre-defined Chart Types 111
Customising a Chart 113
   Drawing a Multiple Column Chart 113
   Changing a Title and an Axis Label 115
   Drawing a Pie Chart 116

10. THE POWERPOINT ENVIRONMENT . . . 119

Starting the PowerPoint Program 119
The PowerPoint Screen 120
PowerPoint Views 123
   Outline View 123
   Slide Sorter View 124
   Notes Pages View 124
   Slide Show View 125
Getting Familiar with PowerPoint 125
Using Help in PowerPoint 126

11. DESIGNING A PRESENTATION 127
- The AutoContent Wizard 127
- The Pick a Look Wizard 131
- Inserting a Clip Art Image 133

12. THE ACCESS DATABASE 135
- Starting Access 137
  - The Welcome to Access Screen 137
- Parts of the Access Screen 138
- Using Help in Access 139
- Database Elements 140

13. CREATING A TABLE 141
- Sorting a Database Table 144
  - Applying a Filter to a Sort 145
- Using a Database Form 146
- Working with Data 147
  - Printing a Table View 149
- Relational Database Design 150
- Relationships 152
- Viewing and Editing Relationships 154
- Creating an Additional Table 155

14. CREATING A QUERY 157
- Types of Queries 159
- The Query Window 160
  - Creating a New Query 161
  - Adding Fields to a Query Window 162
  - Types of Criteria 163
- Combining Criteria 164
  - Using Wildcard Characters in Criteria 166

15. USING FORMS & REPORTS 167
- Using the Form Wizard 167
  - Customising a Form 168
- Using the Report Wizard 170

INDEX 173

1. PACKAGE OVERVIEW

Microsoft Office is a collection of full-featured products with the same look and feel that work together as if they were a single program.

Microsoft Office includes Microsoft Word, Excel, and PowerPoint. The Professional version of Microsoft Office (MS-Office Pro) includes, in addition to the above applications, the fully relational database management system called Access. With both versions of MS-Office you also get a workstation licence for Microsoft Mail.

Microsoft Office applications have a built-in consistency which makes them easier to use. For example, all applications in MS-Office have standardised toolbars and consistent menus, commands, and dialogue boxes. Once you become familiar with one application, it is far easier to learn and use the others.

All MS-Office applications make use of what is known as IntelliSense, which anticipates what you want to do and produces the correct result. For example, AutoCorrect and AutoFormat in Word can, when activated, correct common spelling mistakes and format an entire document automatically, while TipWizard in Excel can give you hints on how to work faster and more efficiently. Other Wizards in all four applications can help you with everyday tasks and/or make complex tasks easier to manage.

With OfficeLinks and OLE 2.0 (Object Linking and Embedding), you can move and share information seamlessly between MS-Office applications. For example, you can drag information from one application to another, and can insert a Microsoft Excel worksheet directly into a Word document by simply clicking a button on a Word toolbar.

Finally, Microsoft Visual Basic for Applications, gives you a powerful and flexible development platform with which to create custom solutions.

Hardware and Software Requirements

If Microsoft Office is already installed on your computer, you can safely skip the rest of this chapter.

To install and use MS-Office, you need an IBM-compatible computer equipped with Intel's 80386sx (or higher) processor. The minimum recommended processor speed is 20 megahertz (MHz). In addition, you need the following:

- MS-DOS version 3.1 or later, plus any one of the following: Microsoft Windows version 3.1, Windows for Workgroups version 3.11, Windows NT or Windows NT Advanced Server version.

- Random access memory (RAM): 4MB; 8MB recommended when running multiple programs.

- Hard disc space available for MS-Office Standard: 21MB for minimum installation; 49MB for typical; 68MB for maximum. For MS-Office Pro: 29MB for minimum installation; 58MB for typical; 82MB for maximum.

- Video adapter: VGA or higher resolution. If you are using PowerPoint, you will need a 256-colour video adapter.

- Pointing device: Microsoft Mouse or compatible.

Realistically, to run MS-Office Pro with reasonable sized applications, you will need a 486 or a Pentium PC with preferably 8MB of RAM. To run Microsoft Office from a network, you must also have a network compatible with your Windows operating environment, such as Microsoft's Windows for Workgroups, Windows NT, LAN Manager, or Novell's NetWare.

To use Microsoft Mail, you must acquire the server version of Microsoft Mail for PC Networks, even though MS-Office includes a client licence. The software required to run Microsoft Mail is included with the server version which must be ordered separately.

Installing MS-Office

Installing MS-Office on your computer's hard disc is made very easy with the use of the SETUP program, which even configures MS-Office automatically to take advantage of the computer's hardware. You need to run the SETUP program because part of its job is to convert compressed Office files from the distribution discs prior to copying them onto your hard disc.

Note: If you are using a virus detection utility, disable it before running SETUP, as it might conflict with it.

To install MS-Office, start Windows, then use the Program Manager's **File, Run** command, as shown below.

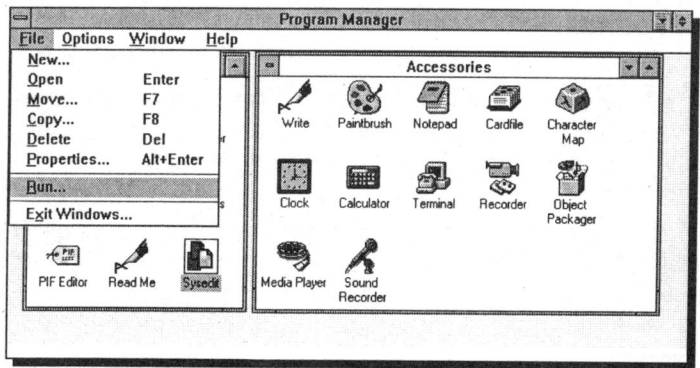

Selecting this command, opens the Run dialogue box:

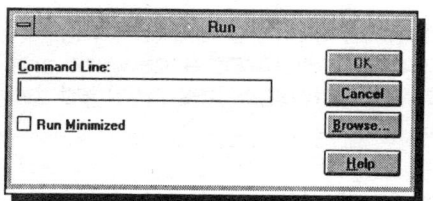

If the application was distributed on diskettes, insert disc #1 into the A: drive and type in the **Command Line** box:

```
a:setup
```

3

Clicking the **OK** button, starts the installation of Microsoft Office. SETUP does the following:

- Asks you to close any open applications.
- Prompts you to type your name and the name of your organisation (optional).
- Prompts you to write down the product ID number on your registration card.
- Prompts you to supply the path to the directory where you want to install Office, and then checks your system and the available hard disc space.

Next, select the type of installation you want. The SETUP program provides four basic options. The available options vary depending on how you are installing Office; directly from discs or CD-ROM, or from the network.

Typical installs the most common features of the Office applications, saving space on the hard disc.

Complete/Custom lets you install all of the Office components, or select only the features you want to install.

Laptop (Minimum) lets you select only the applications you want and installs the minimum required files.

Workstation is only available if you are setting up Office from a network and the network manager has provided the option.

Obviously, depending on the type of set-up, some options may not be available.

If you select **Complete/Custom** installation, the following is displayed:

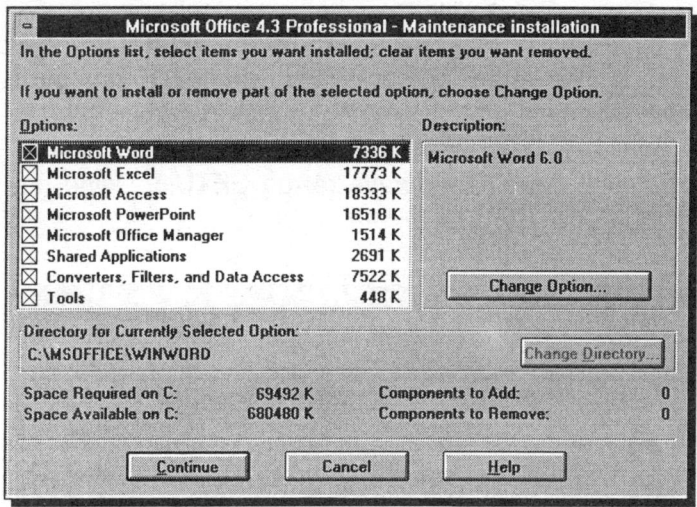

Make sure the check boxes next to the application or component names are selected for all items that you want to install. A selected item displays an "x" in its check box. If you do not want to install an application or component, make sure that its check box is cleared by clicking it. To install all of the applications and all of their components, choose the **Continue** button.

To install part of an application or component, highlight its name by clicking it, then click the **Change Option** button. Clear the check boxes for any options you don't want to install, and then choose the **OK** button. When you finish, choose the **Continue** button.

Depending on the options you select, you may need to respond to additional prompts. Finally, SETUP asks you to select the Windows program group that will contain the Microsoft Office icons, but suggests as a default the name Microsoft Office.

To complete your set-up, you may need to restart Windows, in which case the program returns you to the Program Manager window.

During set-up, the Microsoft Office Manager is added to the Windows StartUp program group so that the Office Manager will start automatically whenever you start Windows.

Should you require to add or remove an Office application, you can always re-run SETUP. Doing so, displays the following screen:

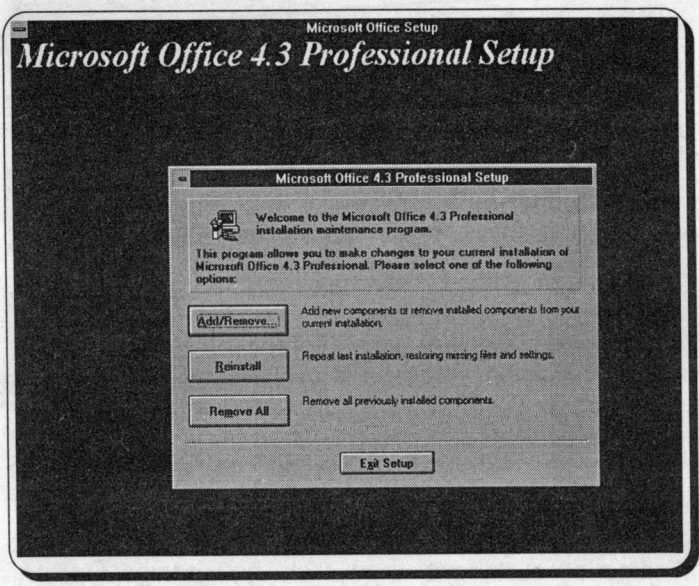

From here you can choose to **Add** or **Remove** components of the package, **Reinstall** by restoring missing files and settings, or **Remove All** previously installed components. Selecting the first option, displays the screen shown on the previous page, from which you can select the components you want to add or remove.

Starting the Program

After MS-Office is installed, the following icon bar appears at the top-right corner of your screen.

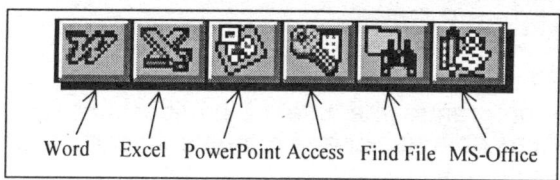

The icons that appear on this toolbar can be changed, or added to, by first clicking the MS-Office icon, then selecting the **Customize** option from the drop-down menu. This displays the Customize dialogue box on which you can select other options by checking the small box against each name. The three tabs on this dialogue box control what appears on the **Toolbar** and the drop-down **Menu**, and what you **View**.

To remove all the icons from your screen, click the MS-Office icon and select **Exit**. Clicking one of the first four icons, starts the appropriate MS-Office application.

MS-Office Program Icons:

MS-Office applications can be started, when Windows is running, from within the **Microsoft Office** group window (shown below) which the SETUP program created in the Program Manager.

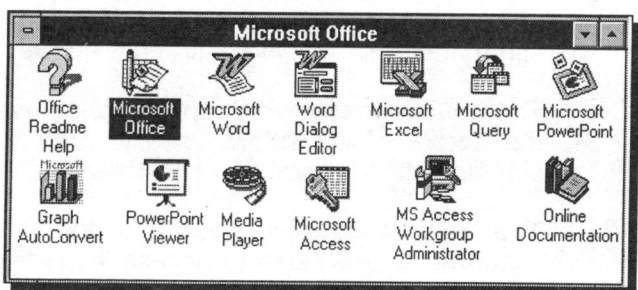

To start any one of the four MS-Office applications, either double-click the appropriate icon in the **Microsoft Office** group window, or double-click an appropriate document file in the Windows File Manager.

The Mouse Pointers

In MS-Office applications, as with all other graphical based programs, the use of a mouse makes many operations both easier and more fun to carry out.

MS-Office makes use of the mouse pointers available in Windows, as illustrated below, which it uses for its various functions. When an MS-Office application is initially started up the first you will see is the hourglass, which turns into an upward pointing hollow arrow once the individual application screen appears on your display. Other shapes depend on the type of work you are doing at the time.

The hourglass which displays when you are waiting while performing a function.

The arrow which appears when the pointer is placed over menus, scrolling bars, and buttons.

The I-beam which appears in normal text areas of the screen.

The large 4-headed arrow which appears after choosing the **Control, Move/Size** command(s) for moving or sizing windows.

The double arrows which appear when over the border of a window, used to drag the side and alter the size of the window.

The Help hand which appears in the Help windows, and is used to access 'hypertext' type links.

MS-Office applications, like other Windows packages, have additional mouse pointers which facilitate the execution of selected commands. Some of these are:

- ▧?   The query pointer which appears on the screen after you click the Help button on the Toolbar. Pointing to a command name or an area on the screen and clicking, allows you to view a Help topic relating to the selected item.

- ↓   The vertical pointer which appears when pointing over a column in a table or worksheet and used to select the column.

- →   The horizontal pointer which appears when pointing at a row in a table or worksheet and used to select the row.

- ◿   The slanted arrow which appears when the pointer is placed in the selection bar area of text or a table.

- ←||→   The vertical split arrow which appears when pointing over the area separating two columns and used to size a column.

- ≑   The horizontal split arrow which appears when pointing over the area separating two rows and used to size a row.

- \+   The frame cross which you drag to create a frame.

- ✎   The draw pointer which appears when you are drawing freehand.

MS-Office has a few additional mouse pointers to the ones above, but their shape is mostly self-evident.

Manipulating Windows

To use MS-Office or any Windows program effectively, you will need to be able to manipulate a series of windows, to select which one is to be active, to move them, or change their size, so that you can see all the relevant parts of each one. What follows is a short discussion on how to manipulate windows.

To help with the illustration of the various points to be discussed shortly, we will create three windows in the Microsoft Word program. To do this, start Word by double-clicking on its icon, then click the **OK** button to close the **Tip of the Day** dialogue box, and click twice the New icon, shown here, to be found at the extreme left on the Word Toolbar, to display three new documents on the screen. When Document3 is displayed, select the **Window, Arrange All** command. The three opened windows then rearrange in tile form, as shown below.

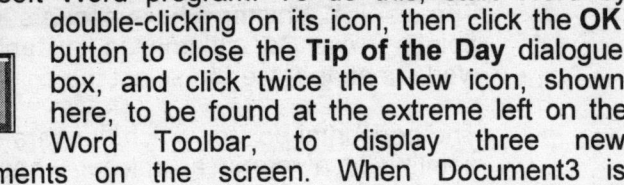

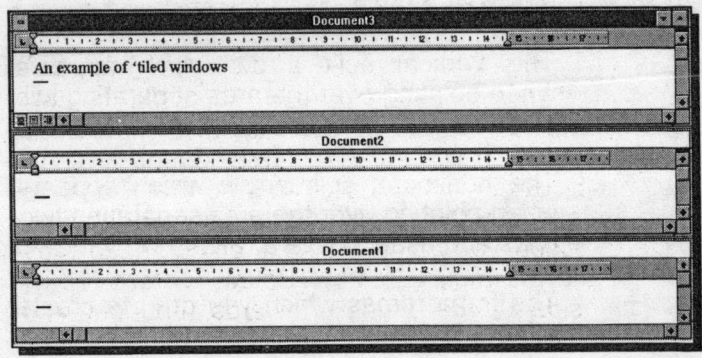

Note: When using MS-Office, it is very easy to open more documents than you need. To conserve memory, check with the **Window** command and close any unwanted documents, by first making them active (see next section), then using the **File, Close** command.

Changing the Active Window:

To make a Document window the active one, point to it and click the left mouse button, or, if you are in full screen mode or the window is obscured, choose the **Window** option of the menu and select its name from the displayed list.

Moving Windows and Dialogue Boxes:

To move a window, or a dialogue box, point to the title bar and drag it (press the left button and keep it pressed while moving the mouse) until the shadow border is where you want it to be (as shown below), then release the mouse button.

Sizing a Window:

To size an active window, move it so that the side you want to change is visible, them place the mouse pointer to the edge of the window or corner so that it changes to a two-headed arrow, then drag the two-headed arrow in the direction you want that side or corner to move and release the mouse button. Below, we are moving the right side of the window towards the right, thus making the window larger.

Minimising and Maximising Windows:

A document window (or an application) can be minimised into an icon at the bottom of the screen. This can be done by clicking the 'Minimise' button (the downward arrow in the upper-right corner of the window).

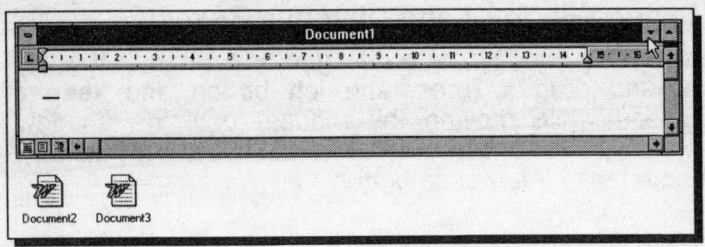

In the above screen dump we show the Document2 and Document3 windows minimised at the bottom of the screen and the mouse pointer pointing at the minimise button of Document1 window.

To maximise a window so that it fills the entire screen, click on the 'Maximise' button (the upward arrow in the upper-right corner of the window).

An application which has been minimised or maximised can be returned to its original size and position on the 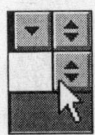 screen by either double-clicking on its icon to expand it to a window, or clicking on the double-headed button in the upper-right corner of the maximised window, shown here, to reduce it to its former size.

Closing a Window:

A document window can be closed at any time to save screen space and memory by double-click on the Control menu button (the large hyphen in the upper-left corner of the window).

If you try to close a window of an application document, such as that of Document1, in which you have made changes since the last time you saved it, you will get a warning in the form of a dialogue box asking confirmation prior to closing it. This safeguards against loss of information.

The Menu Bar Options

Each MS-Office application has its own Menu bar which is situated at the top of the screen, just under the Toolbar (the one that contains the various command icons). Below, we show Word's Menu bar options.

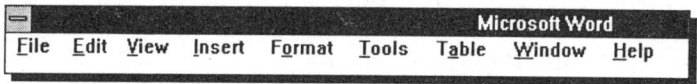

Other MS-Office applications might not have the same options, but learning to access the sub-menus of one, teaches you how to handle the others.

Each Menu bar option has associated with it a pull-down sub-menu. To activate the menu, either press the <Alt> key, which causes the first option of the menu (in this case the **File** option) to be highlighted, then use the right and left arrow keys to highlight any of the other options on the Menu bar, or use the mouse to point to an option. Pressing the <Enter> key, or clicking the left mouse button, reveals the pull-down sub-menu of the highlighted menu option.

The sub-menu of the **File** option is shown below.

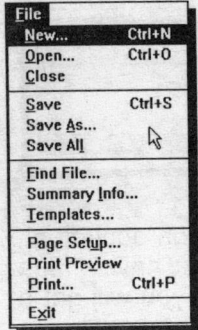

Menu options can also be activated directly by pressing the <Alt> key followed by the underlined letter of the required option. Thus, pressing <Alt+F>, causes the pull-down **File** sub-menu to be displayed. You can use the up and down arrow keys to move the highlighted bar up and down a sub-menu, or the right and left arrow keys to move along the options on the Menu bar.

Note that as you move up and down a sub-menu, the Status bar shows a brief description of the highlighted option. Pressing the <Enter> key, selects the highlighted option. Pressing the <Esc> key once, closes the pull-down sub-menu, while pressing it for a second time, closes the menu system.

Some of the sub-menu options can be accessed with 'quick key' combinations from the keyboard. Such combinations are shown on the drop-down menus, for example, <Ctrl+S> is the quick key for **Save** option in the **File** sub-menu. If a sub-menu option is not available, at any time, it will display in a grey colour.

Shortcut Menus:

If you click the right mouse button on any screen, or document, a shortcut menu is displayed with the most frequently used commands relating to the type of work you are doing at the time.

The screen on the next page shows the shortcut menu that opens when working with Word and the editing area is selected.

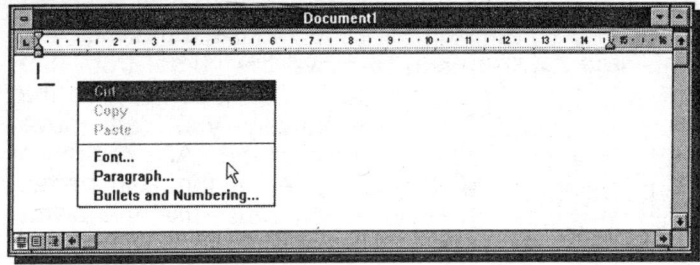

In a similar way, whatever you are doing in an MS-Office application, you have rapid access to a menu of relevant functions by right clicking your mouse. Left clicking the mouse at a menu selection will choose that function.

Dialogue Boxes:

Three periods after a sub-menu option or command, means that a dialogue box will open when the option or command is selected. A dialogue box is used for the insertion of additional information, such as the name of a file or path.

To see a dialogue box, from within Word press <Alt+F>, and select the **Open** option. The 'Open' dialogue box appears on the screen as follows:

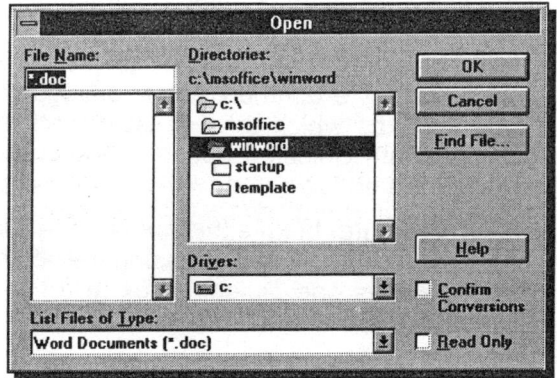

When a dialogue box opens, the easiest way to move around it is by clicking with the mouse, otherwise the <Tab> key can be used to move the cursor from one column in the box to another (<Shift+Tab> moves the cursor backwards), or alternatively you can move directly to a desired field by holding the <Alt> key down and pressing the underlined letter in the field name. Within a column of options you must use the arrow keys to move from one to another.

Having selected an option or typed in information, you must press a command button such as the **OK** or **Cancel** button, or choose from additional options. To select the **OK** button with the mouse, simply point and click, while with the keyboard you must first press the <Tab> key until the dotted rectangle moves to the required button, and then press the <Enter> key. Pressing <Enter> at any time while a dialogue box is open, will cause the marked items to be selected and the box to be closed.

Some dialogue boxes contain List boxes which show a column of available choices (similar to the one at the bottom of the previous screen dump which appeared by pressing the down-arrow button). If there are more choices than can be seen in the area provided, use the scroll bars to reveal them. To select a single item from a List box, either double-click the item, or use the arrow keys to highlight the item and press <Enter>.

Other dialogue boxes contain Option buttons with a list of mutually exclusive items. The default choice is marked with a black dot against its name, while unavailable options are dimmed. Other dialogue boxes contain Check boxes which offer a list of options you can switch on or off. Selected options show a cross in the box against the option name.

To cancel a dialogue box, either press the **Cancel** button, or press the <Esc> key. Pressing the <Esc> key in succession, closes one dialogue box at a time, and eventually aborts the menu option.

2. THE WORD WORD PROCESSOR

Starting the Program

Word is started in Windows either by double-clicking the left mouse button on the 'Microsoft Word' icon, or by double-clicking on a Word document file (with the extension .doc) in the Windows File Manager. In the latter case the document will be loaded into Word at the same time.

The first time you start Word you get the 'Tip of the Day' window displayed. You could easily spend a lot of time reading the numerous useful tips by clicking at the **Next Tip** button.

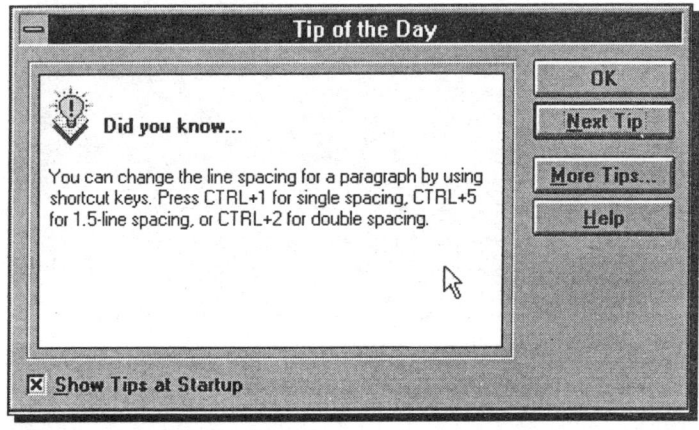

If you would like a different tip to appear every time you start Word, then place the mouse pointer on the little square at the bottom of the window and click the left mouse button to check it. If this box is not checked, the Tip of the Day window will not appear on start-up. The choice is yours.

Getting Familiar with Word

Word has two options under the **Help** menu which allow you to familiarise yourself with the package; **Quick Preview** and **Examples and Demos**.

The first one of these, is a show tutorial. To access it, use the **Help, Quick Preview** command which displays:

This tutorial is a good introduction to the powerful features of Word. It takes about half an hour to work through and is well worth the time. You can of course run through the different options as often as you like, and not necessarily in the presentation order. When you have finished, press the **Return to Word** button.

The second familiarisation option offers detailed information on a number of selected topics, and has the added ability of letting you practise on them. To access this option, start Word and use the **Help, Examples and Demos** command, which causes the following screen to be displayed.

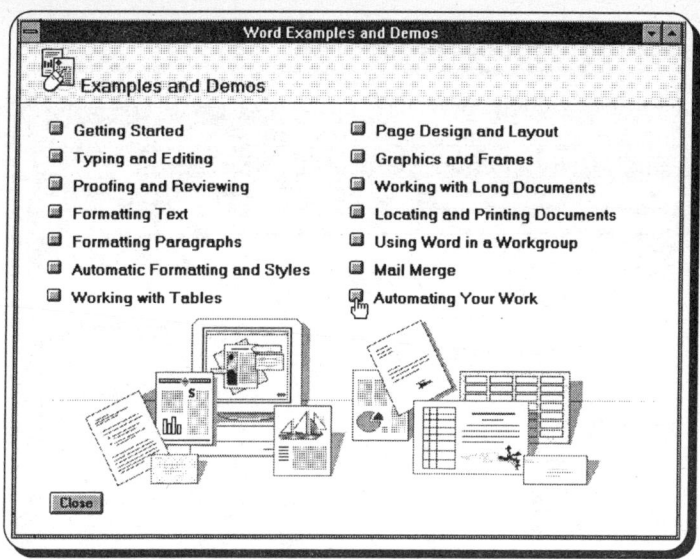

As you can see from the list above, this option gives you far more detailed information on a much larger selection of topics. We suggest you return to this option often to build up your knowledge of the package.

The Word Screen

The opening 'blank' screen of Word for Windows is shown overleaf. It is perhaps worth spending some time looking at the various parts that make up this screen. Word follows the usual Microsoft Windows conventions and if you are familiar with these you can skip through this section. Otherwise a few minutes might be well spent here.

The window as shown takes up the full screen area available. If you click on the application restore button, the top one of the two restore buttons at the top right of the screen, you can make Word show in a smaller window. This can be useful when you are running several applications at the same time and you want to transfer between them with the mouse.

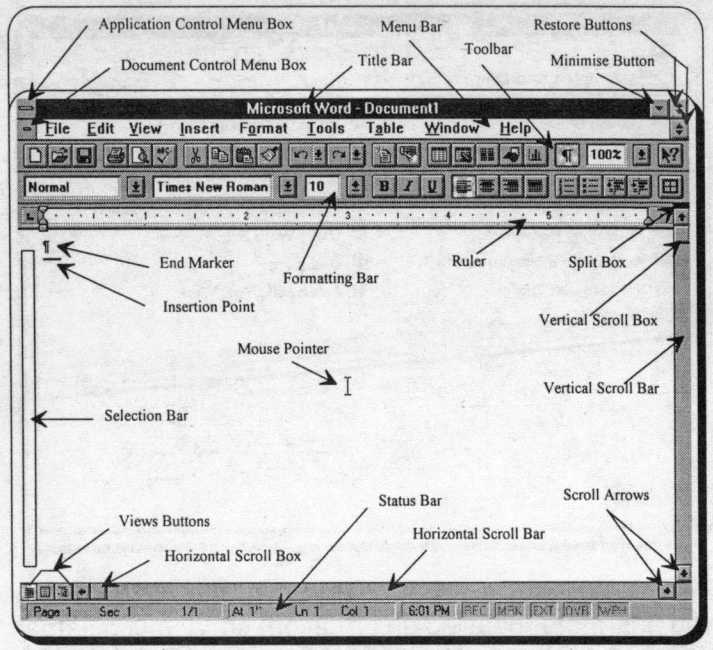

Note that the Word window, which in this case displays an empty document with the title 'Document1', has a solid 'Title bar', indicating that it is the active application window. Although multiple windows can be displayed simultaneously, you can only enter data into the active window (which will always be displayed on top). Title bars of non active windows appear a lighter shade than that of the active one.

The Word screen is divided into several areas which have the following functions:

Area	*Function*
Control Boxes	Clicking on the top control menu box, displays the pull-down Control menu which can be used to control the program window. It includes commands for re-sizing,

moving, maximising, minimising, switching to another task, and closing the window. The lower menu box controls the current document window in the same manner.

Title Bar The bar at the top of a window which displays the application name and the name of the current document.

Menu Bar The bar below the Title bar which allows you to choose from several menu options. Clicking on a menu item displays the pull-down menu associated with that item.

Toolbar The bar below the Menu bar which contains buttons that give you mouse click access to the functions most often used in the program. These are grouped according to function, for example, the first three buttons deal with file manipulation, the next four with editing functions, etc.

Restore Buttons When clicked on, these buttons restore the active window to the position and size occupied before being maximised or minimised. The restore button is then replaced by a Maximise button, with a single up-pointing arrow, which can be used to set the window to its former size.

Minimise Box The button you point to and click to store an application as an icon (small symbol) at the bottom of the screen. Double clicking on such an icon will restore the screen.

Formatting Bar	The buttons on the Formatting Bar allow you to change the attributes of a font, such as italic and underline, and also to format text in various ways. The Formatting Bar contains three boxes; a style box, a font box and a size box which show which style, font and size of characters are currently being used. These boxes give access to other installed styles, fonts and character sizes.
Ruler	The area where you can see and set tabulation points and indents.
Split Box	The area to the extreme right of the Ruler which when dragged allows you to split the screen.
Scroll Bars	The areas on the screen (extreme right and bottom of each window) that contain scroll boxes in vertical and horizontal bars. Clicking on these bars allows you to control the part of a document which is visible on the screen.
Scroll Arrows	The arrowheads at each end of each scroll bar at which you can click to scroll the screen up and down one line, or left and right 10% of the screen, at a time.
Selection Bar	The area on the screen in the left margin of the Word window (marked here with a box for convenience), where the mouse pointer changes to an arrow that slants to the right. Clicking the left mouse once selects the current line, while clicking twice selects the current paragraph.

Views Buttons   Clicking these buttons changes screen views quickly.

Status Bar   The bottom line of the screen that displays information relating to your document, and in which a short description appears on what a button does when you point and click at it.

For a brief description on how to action the various Menu bar options and what they do when executed, refer to the end of Chapter 1. Obviously, the Menu bar options differ slightly from one MS-Office application to the next, but their general form and behaviour remains the same.

The Formatting Bar:

This is located below the Toolbar at the top of the Word for Windows screen and is divided into seven sections, as shown below. These can only be accessed by clicking on them with the left mouse button.

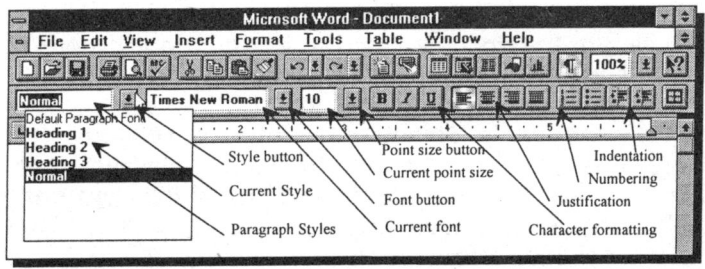

The Current Style box on the left of the Character formatting buttons, shows the style of the current paragraph; the one containing the cursor. By clicking the down-arrow button next to it, a list of all the available styles in the active template is produced (as shown). Clicking on one of these will change the style of the current paragraph.

To the right of the Style button is the Current font box which shows the current typeface. Clicking on the down-arrow button to the right of it allows you to change the typeface of any selected text. The Current point size box shows the size of selected characters. This size can be changed by clicking on the down-arrow button next to it and selecting another size from the displayed list.

Next, are three Character formatting buttons which allow you to enhance selected text by emboldening, italicising, or underlining it. The next four buttons allow you to change the justification of a selected paragraph, while the next four help you set the different types of Numbering and Indentation options. The last button allows you to add borders and shading to selected paragraphs, table cells and frames.

The Status Bar:

This is located at the bottom of the Word window and is used to display statistics about the active document. For example, when a document is being opened, the Status bar displays for a short time its name and length in terms of total number of characters. Once a document is opened, the Status bar displays the statistics of the document at the insertion point; here it is on Page 2, Section 1, 1 character from the left margin. Double-clicking the left of the status bar displays the Go To dialogue box. There is even help for WordPerfect users converting to Word. To activate this facility, use the **Help** command, click the **Options** button in the displayed dialogue box, and check the **Help for WordPerfect Users** box.

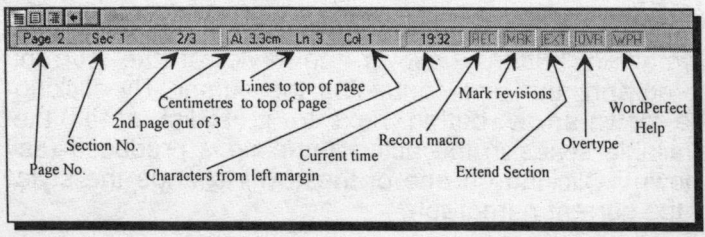

Using Help in Word

Using the Microsoft Windows Help Program, Word provides on-line Help for every function. You can re-size, move, tile, or cascade the Help window and the current document so that you can keep both of them displayed at the same time.

Help topics can be printed on paper by selecting the topic, then using Help's **File, Print Topic** command, as shown below.

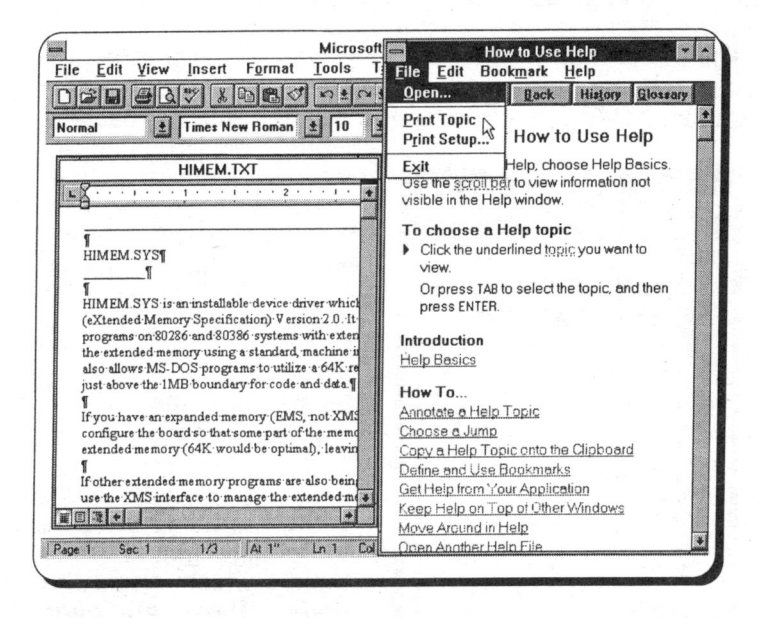

In addition, there are several ways to obtain on-line Help. These are:

On-line Help Messages: Word displays a command description in the Status bar when you choose a menu or command.

Context Sensitive Help: Simply press **F1** to get instant help on any menu function that you are carrying out. If you are not using a menu box you will bring up the Help Contents window. Selecting the **File, Exit** command (<Alt+F> followed by X), will close the Help window and return you to your original screen. The <Alt+F4> quick key combination may also be used to exit Help.

Another way of getting context sensitive help is to click the Help button on the Toolbar, shown here, then move the modified mouse pointer to an area of the document or on to a particular Toolbar button and press the left mouse button.

The Help Menu: Choose **Help**, to display the menu, then choose **Index** to display the Word Help Index shown here. Clicking one of the letter buttons, causes Word Help to jump to the relevant part of the listing which starts with the chosen letter. With the keyboard, press <Tab> to select the desired letter, then press <Enter>.

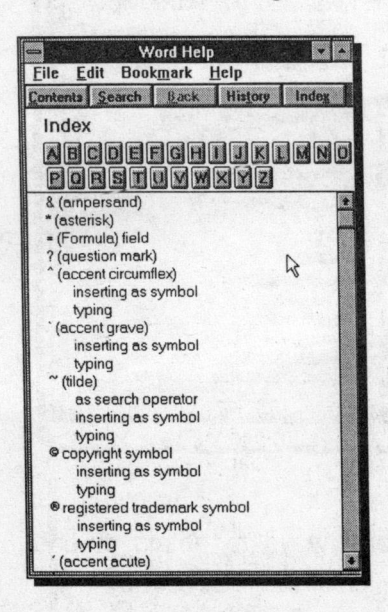

Most of the Word manual contents are in it; you just have to find them. Many Help topics contain cross-references to other related Help topics, which display in green. These are often known as 'hypertext' links, and clicking the hand pointer on them displays their content.

3. WORD DOCUMENT BASICS

When the program is first used, all Word's features default to those shown on page 20. It is quite possible to use Word in this mode, without changing any main settings, but obviously it is possible to customise the package to your exact needs, as we shall see later.

Entering Text

In order to illustrate some of Word's capabilities, you need to have a short text at hand. We suggest you type the memo displayed below into a new document. At this stage, don't worry if the length of the lines below differ from those on your display.

As you type in text, any time you want to force a new line, or paragraph, just press <Enter>. While typing within a paragraph, Word sorts out line lengths automatically (known as 'word wrap'), without you having to press any keys to move to a new line. If you make a mistake while typing, press the <BkSp> key enough times to erase the mistake and start again.

MEMO TO PC USERS
Networked Computers
The microcomputers in the DP room are a mixture of IBM compatible 486 machines of varying speed, memory and hard disc capacity. Each machine is equipped with a 3.5" floppy disc drive of 1.44MB capacity, so that you can save your data on your own diskette.

The computer you are using will have at least a 250MB hard disc on which a number of software packages have been installed. To make life easier, the hard disc is highly structured with each package installed in a separate directory. When the computer is first switched on, the following prompt is displayed on your screen:

    C:\>

Moving Around a Document

You can move the cursor around a document with the normal direction keys, and with the key combinations listed below.

To move	*Press*
Left one character	←
Right one character	→
Up one line	↑
Down one line	↓
Left one word	Ctrl+←
Right one word	Ctrl+→
To beginning of line	Home
To end of line	End
To paragraph beginning	Ctrl+↑
To paragraph end	Ctrl+↓
Up one screen	PgUp
Down one screen	PgDn
To top of previous page	Ctrl+PgUp
To top of next page	Ctrl+PgDn
To beginning of file	Ctrl+Home
To end of file	Ctrl+End

In a multi-page document, use the **Edit**, **Go To** command (or <Ctrl+G>), to jump to a specified page number.

Obviously, you need to become familiar with the above methods of moving the cursor around a document, particularly if you are not using a mouse and you spot an error in a document which needs to be corrected, which is the subject of the next chapter.

Templates and Paragraph Styles

When you start Word for the first time, the Style Status box (at the extreme left of the Formatting bar) contains the word **Normal**. This means that all the text you have entered, at the moment, is shown in the Normal paragraph style which is one of the styles available in the NORMAL template. Every document produced by Word has to use a template, and NORMAL is the default. A template contains, both the document page settings and a set of formatting instructions which can be applied to text.

Changing Paragraph Styles:

To change the style of a paragraph, do the following:

- Place the cursor (insertion pointer) on the paragraph in question, say the title line
- Left click the Style Status button, and select the **Heading 1** style.

The selected paragraph reformats instantly in bold, and in Arial typeface of point size 14.

With the cursor in the second line of text, select **Heading 3** which reformats the line in bold, and Times New Roman point size 12. Your memo should look quite presentable now, as shown below.

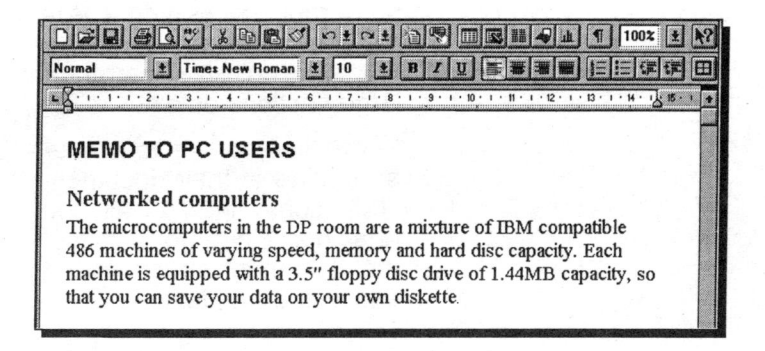

MEMO TO PC USERS

Networked computers

The microcomputers in the DP room are a mixture of IBM compatible 486 machines of varying speed, memory and hard disc capacity. Each machine is equipped with a 3.5" floppy disc drive of 1.44MB capacity, so that you can save your data on your own diskette.

Document Screen Displays

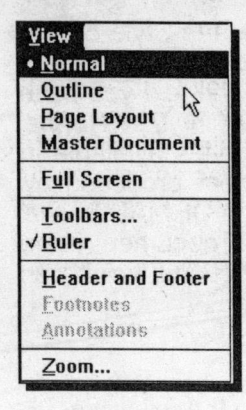

```
View
• Normal
  Outline
  Page Layout
  Master Document
  Full Screen
  Toolbars...
√ Ruler
  Header and Footer
  Footnotes
  Annotations
  Zoom...
```

Word provides four display modes, Normal, Outline, Page Layout, and Master Document, as well as the options to view your documents in a whole range of screen enlargements by selecting **Zoom**. You control all these viewing options with the **View** sub-menu, shown here, and when a document is displayed you can switch freely between them. When first loaded the screen displays in Normal mode.

Selecting the other mode options has the following effect:

Normal — Returns you to normal viewing from either Outline or Page Layout viewing mode.

Outline — Provides a collapsible view of a document, which enables you to see its organisation at a glance. You can display all the text in a file, or just the text that uses the paragraph styles you specify. Using this mode, allows you to quickly rearrange large sections of text.

Some people like to create an outline of their document first, consisting of all the headings, then to sort out the document structure and finally fill in the text.

Page Layout   Provides a WYSIWYG (what you see is what you get) view of a document. The text displays in the typefaces and point sizes you specify, and with the selected attributes (alignment, indention, spacing, etc.). All frames, tables, graphics, headers, footers, and footnotes appear on the screen as they will in the final printed document.

Master Document   Provides you with an outline view of a document that takes its contents from one or more Word documents. For example, each chapter of a book could be made into a sub-document of such a Master Document. The Master Document could then be used to reorganise, add or remove sub-documents. Selecting this mode, causes Word to display the Master Document and Outline toolbars.

Full Screen   Presents you with a clean, uncluttered screen; the Toolbars, Ruler, Scroll bars, and Status bar are removed. To return to the usual screen, click the 'Full' icon, shown here, which appears at the bottom of your screen when in this mode.

Zoom Allows you to change the viewing magnification factor from its default value of 100%. This can also be changed by clicking the 'Zoom Control' icon on the Toolbar. Clicking its down arrow button, reveals other magnification factors, as shown here.

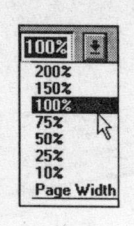

Changing Default Options

Modifying Margins:

To change the standard page margins for your entire document from the cursor position onward, or for selected text (more about this later), do the following:

- Select the **File, Page Setup** command
- Click the left mouse button at the **Margins** tab on the displayed dialogue box, shown below.

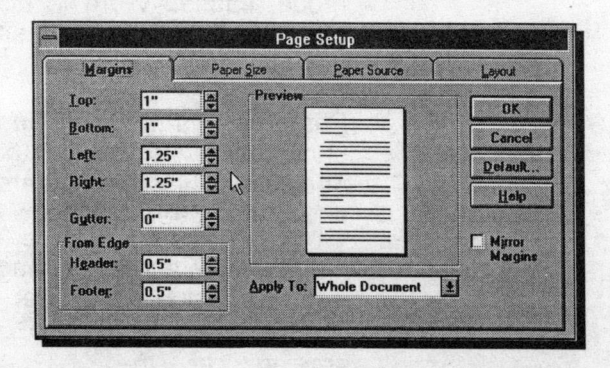

The 'Preview' page in the middle of the box shows how your changes will look on a real page.

Changing the Default Paper Size:

To change the default paper size from Letter (the standard American page size) to A4 (the standard British page size), do the following:

- Select the **File, Page Setup** command
- Click the left mouse button at the **Paper Size** tab on the displayed dialogue box, shown below
- Click the down-arrow against the **Paper Size** box to reveal the list of available paper sizes
- Change the page size as shown below, and press the **Default** button and confirm that you wish this change to affect all new documents based on the NORMAL template.

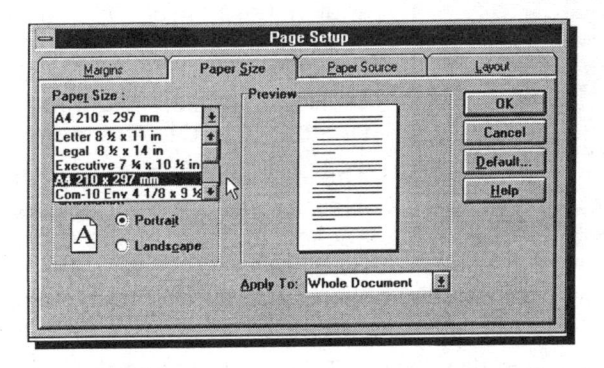

Check that the paper size matches that in your printer, otherwise you may get strange results. The orientation of the printed page is normally **Portrait** (text prints across the page width), but you could choose to change this to **Landscape** which prints across the page length, as long as your printer can print in landscape.

Modifying the Paper Source:

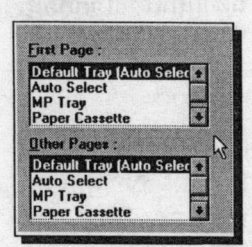

Clicking on the third Page Setup tab, displays yet another dialogue box, part of which is shown here, from which you can select the paper source. You might have a printer that holds paper in trays, in which case you might want to specify that the first page (headed paper perhaps), should be taken from one tray, while the rest of the paper should be taken from a different tray.

Modifying the Page Layout:

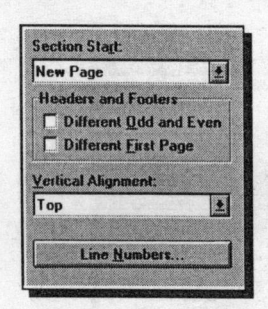

Clicking the last Page Setup tab displays the Layout dialogue box, part of which is shown here. From this dialogue box you can set options for headers and footers, section breaks, vertical alignment and whether to add line numbers.

The default for **Section Sta_r_t** is 'New Page' which allows the section to start at the top of the next page. Pressing the down arrow against this option, allows you to change this choice.

In the Headers and Footers box you can specify whether you want one header or footer for even-numbered pages and a different header or footer for odd-numbered pages. You can further specify if you want a different header or footer on the first page from the header or footer used for the rest of the document. Word can align the top line with the 'Top' margin, but this can be changed with the **_V_ertical Alignment** option.

Changing Other Default Options:

You can also change the default options available to you in Word for Windows, by selecting the **Tools, Options** command. Using the displayed Options dialogue box (shown below) you can:

- Specify the default **View** options. For example, you can select whether non-printing characters, such as Tabs, Spaces, and Paragraph marks, are shown or not.

- Adjust the **General** Word settings, such as the colour of text and its background, and the units of measure from inches to centimetres.

- Adjust the **Print** settings, such as the **Reverse Print Order** mode, or choose to print the **Summary Info** or **Annotations**.

- Change the **Save** options, such as selecting the **Always Create Backup Copy** option for your work.

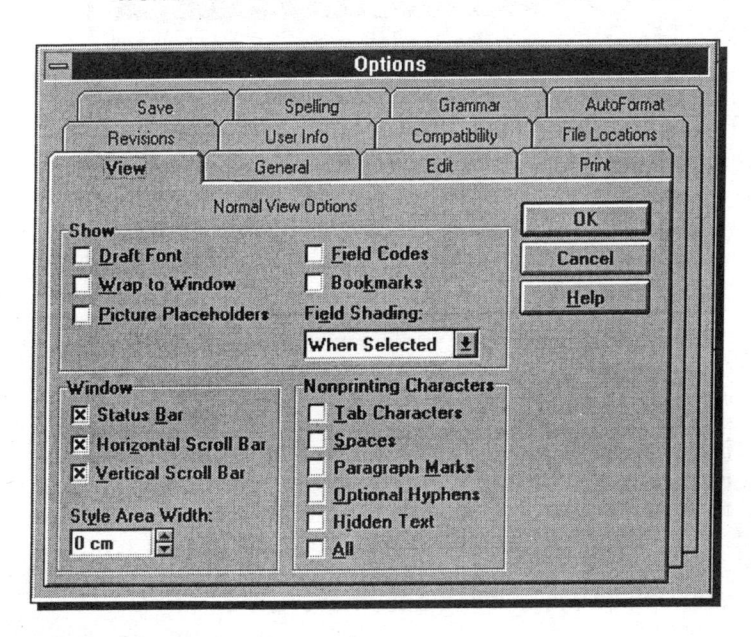

Saving to a File

To save a document to disc, use either of the following two commands:

- **File, Save** which is used when a document has previously been saved to disc in a named file; using this command automatically saves your work under the existing filename without prompting you.

- **File, Save As** command which is used when you want to save your document with a different name from the one you gave it already.

Using the **File, Save As** command (or the very first time you use the **File, Save** command when a document has no name), causes the following dialogue box to appear on your screen:

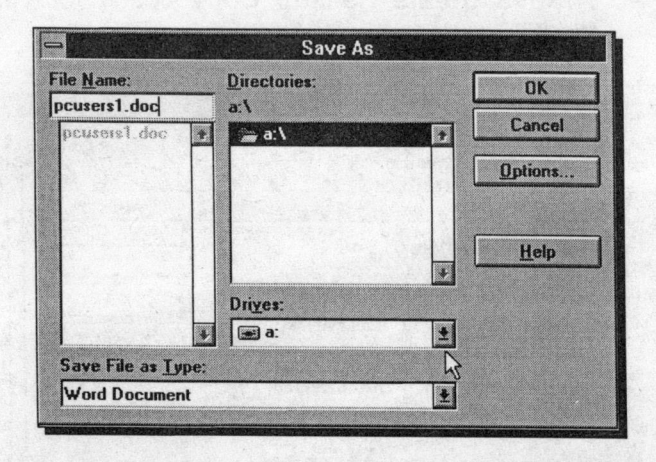

Note that the old document name is highlighted in the **File Name** field box and the program is waiting for you to type a new name. Any name you type (don't use more than 8 characters and don't bother to type the .doc extension, as the program adds it automatically) will replace the existing document name.

You can select a drive other than the one displayed, by clicking the down arrow against the **Drives** field. To save your work currently in memory, move the cursor into the **File Name** box, and type **pcusers1**.

By clicking the **Save File as Type** button at the bottom of the Save As dialogue box, you can save the Document Template, or the Text Only parts of your work, or you can save your document in a variety of other formats, such as DOS Text, ASCII, Rich Text Format, or a number of WordPerfect, Word for Windows, and Word for DOS formats, as well as in Excel and Windows Write formats. All these different formats are saved with appropriate extensions which are recognised by the packages in question.

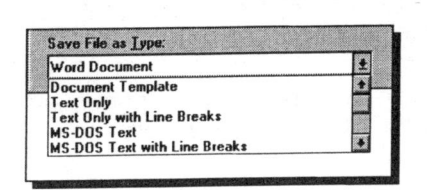

A useful feature in Word is the facility to add a document description to every file by selecting the **File, Summary Info** command. A box, as shown below, opens for you to type additional information about your document.

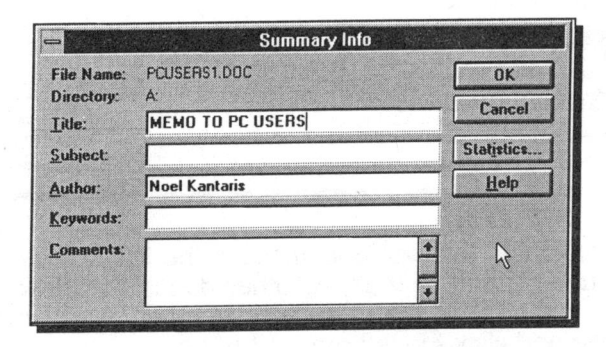

To do this on a more regular basis, make sure that the **Prompt for Summary Info** box in the Save Options dialogue box is selected and appears checked.

Closing a Document:

There are several ways to close a document in Word. Once you have saved it you can double click on the Document Control button at the left end of the menu bar; you would usually use this method when you have several files open together.

If you want to open a new, or another, document you could use the following commands:

- **File, Close** to close the current document (remove it from your computer's memory) before using either
- **File, New** to create a new file, or
- **File, Open** to use an existing file.

If the document (or file) has changed since the last time it was saved, you will be given the option to save it before it is removed from memory.

If a document is not closed before a new document is opened, then both documents will be held in memory, but only one will be the current document. To find out which documents are held in memory, use the **Window** command to reveal the following drop down menu:

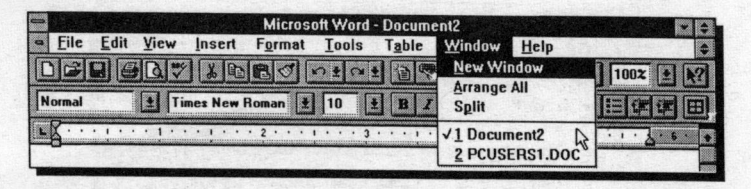

In this case, the first document in the list is the current document, and to make another document the current one, either type the document number, or point at its name and click the left mouse button.

To close a document which is not the current document, use the **Window** command, make it current, and then use the **File, Close** command.

4. EDITING WORD DOCUMENTS

It will not be long, when using Word, before you will need to edit your document. This could include deleting unwanted words, correcting a mistake or adding extra text in the document. All these operations are very easy to carry out.

For small deletions, such as letters or words, the easiest method to adopt is the use of the <Del> or <BkSp> keys. With the <Del> key, position the cursor on the first letter you want to delete and press <Del>; the letter is deleted and the following text moves one space to the left. With the <BkSp> key, position the cursor immediately to the right of the character to be deleted and press <BkSp>; the cursor moves one space to the left pulling the rest of the line with it and overwriting the character to be deleted. Note that the difference between the two is that with <Del> the cursor does not move at all.

Word processing is usually carried out in the insert mode. Any characters typed will be inserted at the cursor location (insertion point) and the following text will be pushed to the right, and down, to make room. To insert blank lines in your text, place the cursor at the beginning of the line where the blank line is needed and press <Enter>. To remove the blank line, position the cursor at its leftmost end and press <Del>.

When larger scale editing is needed you have several alternatives with Word. You can use the **Cut, Copy** and **Paste** operations, after first 'selecting' the text to be altered. These functions are then available when the **Edit** sub-menu is activated. Instead of using the sub-menu you can click on Toolbar button alternatives for all the editing commands. This makes working with a mouse very much easier and quicker. A method, new to later versions of Word is to use the 'drag' facility for copying or moving text.

Selecting Text

The procedure in Word, as with most Windows based applications, is first to select the text to be altered before any operation, such as formatting or editing, can be carried out on it. Selected text is highlighted on the screen. This can be carried out in two main ways:

A. *Using the keyboard, to select:*

- A block of text. Position the cursor on the first character to be selected and hold down the <Shift> key while using the arrow keys to highlight the required text, then release the <Shift> key.

- From the present cursor position to the end of the line. Use <Shift+End>.

- From the present cursor position to the beginning of the line. Use <Shift+Home>.

- From the present cursor position to the end of the document. Use <Shift+Ctrl+End>.

- From the present cursor position to the beginning of the document. Use <Shift+Ctrl+Home>.

B. With the mouse, to select:

- A block of text.

    Press down the left mouse button at the beginning of the block and while holding it pressed, drag the cursor across the block so that the desired text is highlighted, then release the mouse button.

- A word.

    Double-click at the word.

- A line.

    Place the mouse pointer on the selection bar, just to the left of the line, and click once (for multiple lines, after selecting the first line, drag the pointer in the selection bar).

- A sentence.

    Hold the <Ctrl> key down and click in the sentence.

- A paragraph.

    Place the mouse pointer in the selection bar and double-click (for multiple paragraphs, after selecting the first paragraph, drag the pointer in the selection bar).

- The whole document.

    Place the mouse pointer in the selection bar, hold the <Ctrl> key down and click once.

Copying Blocks of Text

Once text has been selected it can be copied to another location in your present document, to another Word document, or to another Windows application, via the clipboard. As with most of the editing and formatting operations there are several alternative ways of doing this, as follows:

- Use the **Edit, Copy** command sequence from the menu, to copy the selected text to the Windows clipboard, moving the cursor to the start of where you want the copied text to be placed, and using the **Edit, Paste** command.

- Use the quick key combinations, <Ctrl+Ins> (or <Ctrl+C>) to copy and <Shift+Ins> (or <Ctrl+V>) to paste, once the text to be copied has been selected, which does not require the menu bar to be activated.

- Use the 'Copy to clipboard' and 'Paste from clipboard' Toolbar buttons; you can of course only use this method with a mouse.

  To copy the same text again to another location, on to any open window document or application, move the cursor to the new location and paste it there with any of these methods, as it is stored on the clipboard until it is replaced by the next Cut, or Copy operation.

- First select the text, then hold both the <Ctrl> and <Shift> keys depressed, place the cursor at the start of where you want the copied text to be and press the right mouse button. The new text will insert itself where placed, even if the overstrike mode is in operation. Text copied by this method is not placed on the clipboard, so multiple copies are not possible, as with the other methods.

Moving Blocks of Text

Selected text can be moved to any location in the same document by either of the following:

- Using the **Edit, Cut,** command or <Shift+Del> (or <Ctrl+X>).
- Clicking the 'Cut to clipboard' Toolbar button, shown here.

Next, move the cursor to the required new location and use either of the following procedures:

- The **Edit, Paste** command.
- Any other paste actions as described previously.

The moved text will be placed at the cursor location and will force any existing text to make room for it. This operation can be cancelled by simply pressing <Esc>. Once moved, multiple copies of the same text can be produced by other **Paste** operations.

Selected text can be moved by dragging the mouse with the left button held down. The drag pointer is an arrow with an attached square - the vertical dotted line showing the point of insertion.

Deleting Blocks of Text

When text is 'cut' it is removed from the document, but placed on the clipboard until further text is either copied or cut. With Word any selected text can be deleted by pressing **Edit, Cut,** or by pressing the <Del>, or <BkSp> keys. However, using **Edit, Cut**, allows you to use the **Edit, Paste** command, but using the <Del> or <BkSp> keys, does not.

The Undo Command

As text is lost with the delete command you should use it with caution, but if you do make a mistake all is not lost as long as you act promptly. The **Edit, Undo** command or <Ctrl+Z> (or <Alt+BkSp>) reverses your most recent editing or formatting commands.

You can also use the Toolbar buttons, shown here, to undo one of several editing or formatting mistakes (press the down arrow to the right of the left button to see a list of your changes) or even redo any one of the undo moves with the right button.

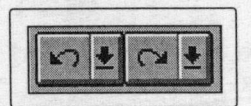

Undo does not reverse any action once editing changes have been saved to file. Only editing done since the last save can be reversed.

Finding and Changing Text

Word allows you to search for specifically selected text, or character combinations. To do this use:

- The **Find** or the **Replace** option from the **Edit** command sub-menu.

Using the **Find** option (<Ctrl+F>), will highlight each occurrence of the supplied text in turn so that you can carry out some action on it, such as change its font or appearance.

Using the **Replace** option (<Ctrl+H>), allows you to specify what replacement is to be automatically carried out. For example, in a long article you may decide to replace every occurrence of the word 'microcomputers' with the word 'PCs'.

To illustrate the **Replace** procedure, either select the option from the **Edit** sub-menu or use the quick key combination <Ctrl+H>. This opens the Replace dialogue box, displayed on the top half of the composite screen dump shown below.

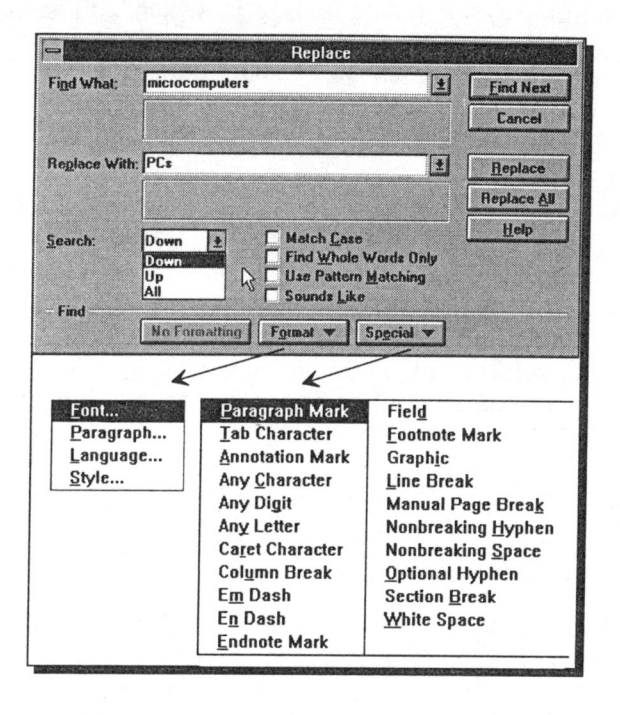

Towards the bottom of the dialogue box, there are four check boxes with which you can match the case of letters in the search string, and/or a whole word. The last two check boxes can be used for a pattern, or 'sounds like' matching.

The two buttons, **Format** and **Special**, situated at the bottom of the dialogue box, let you control how the search is carried out. The lists of available options, when either of these buttons is pressed, are displayed in the above composite screen dump.

You can force both the search and the replace operations to work with exact text attributes. For example, selecting:

- The **Font** option from the list under **Format**, displays a dialogue box in which you select a font (such as Arial, Times New Roman, etc.); a font-style (such as regular, bold, italic, etc.); an underline option (such as single, double, etc.); and special effects (such as strike-through, superscript, subscript, etc.).

- The **Paragraph** option, lets you control indentation, spacing (before and after), and alignment.

- The **Style** option, allows you to search for, or replace, different paragraph styles. This can be useful if you develop a new style and want to change all the text of another style in a document to use your preferred style.

With the use of the **Special** button, you can search for, and replace, various specified document marks, tabs, hard returns, etc., or a combination of both these and text, as listed in the previous screen dump.

Below we list only two of the many key combinations of special characters that could be typed into the **Find What** and **Replace With** boxes when the **Use Pattern Matching** box is checked.

Type	*To find or replace*
?	Any single character within a pattern. For example, searching for nec?, will find necessary, neck, connect, etc.
*	Any string of characters. For example, searching for c*r, will find such words as cellar, character, chillier, etc.

The above will not work unless the **Use Pattern Matching** box is checked.

Page Breaks

The program automatically inserts a 'soft' page break in a document when a page of typed text is full. To force a manual, or hard page break, either type <Ctrl+Enter> or use the **Insert**, **Break** command and select **Page Break** in the dialogue box, as shown below.

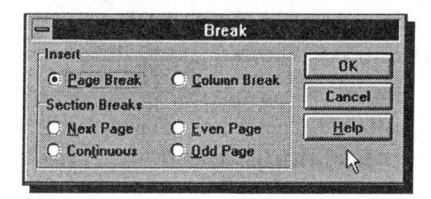

Pressing **OK** places a series of dots across the page to indicate the page break, as shown below. To delete manual page breaks place the cursor on the selection bar to the left of the page break mark, click once to highlight the line of dots, and press <Del>.

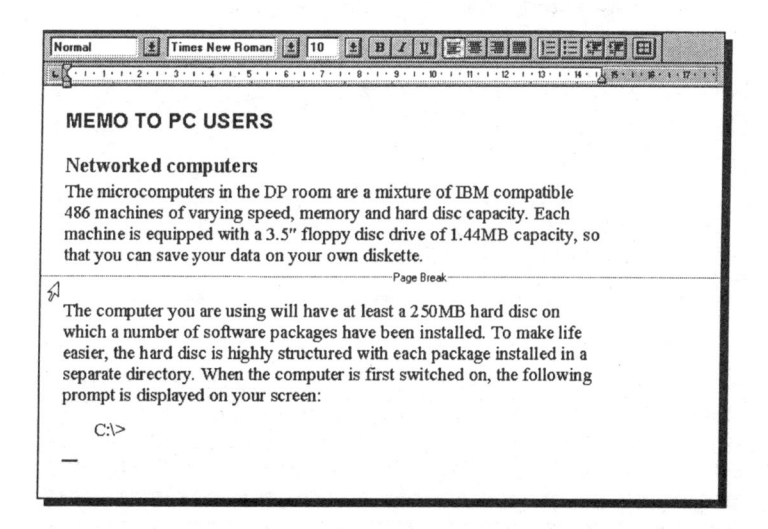

MEMO TO PC USERS

Networked computers

The microcomputers in the DP room are a mixture of IBM compatible 486 machines of varying speed, memory and hard disc capacity. Each machine is equipped with a 3.5" floppy disc drive of 1.44MB capacity, so that you can save your data on your own diskette.

―――――――――――――――― Page Break ――――――――――――――――

The computer you are using will have at least a 250MB hard disc on which a number of software packages have been installed. To make life easier, the hard disc is highly structured with each package installed in a separate directory. When the computer is first switched on, the following prompt is displayed on your screen:

C:\>

Soft page breaks which are automatically entered by the program at the end of pages, cannot be deleted.

Using the Spell Checker

The package has a very comprehensive spell checker and has the ability to add specialised and personal dictionaries. The main dictionary contains more that 100,000 words which cannot be edited. The user dictionary you can customise and edit. If you are using personal dictionaries and you use the spell checker and choose **Add**, Word adds the word to the specified user dictionary, which should have the file extension .dic.

To spell check your document, either click the 'Spelling' button on the Standard Toolbar, shown here, or use the **Tools**, **Spelling** command (or **F7**) to open the dialogue box shown below.

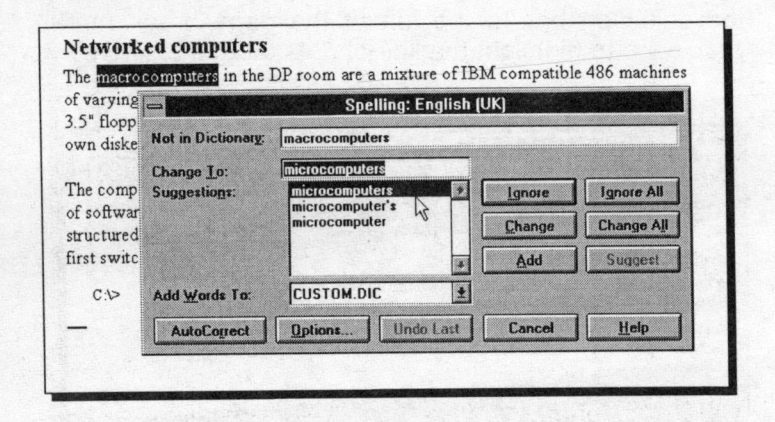

Word starts spell checking from the point of insertion onwards. If you want to check a word or paragraph only, highlight it first. If you want to spell check the whole document, move the insertion point to the beginning of the document before starting. Once Word has found a misspelled word, you can correct it in the **Change To** box, or select a word from the **Suggestions** list.

Printing Documents

When Windows was first installed on your computer the printers you intend to use should have been selected, and the SETUP program should have installed the appropriate printer drivers. Before printing for the first time, you would be wise to ensure that your printer is in fact properly installed. To do this, open the Windows Control Panel and double-click the 'Printers' icon, which opens the **Printers** dialogue box shown below.

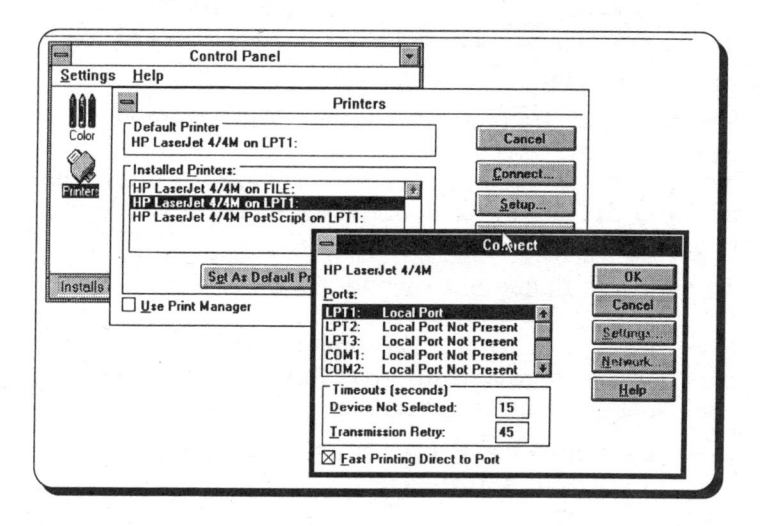

Here, two printer drivers have been installed; an HP LaserJet 4/4M as the 'default' printer configured to either output to a printer via the parallel port LPT1, or to a disc file, and an HP LaserJet 4/4M PostScript, also configured to output to a printer. Your selections may, obviously, not be the same.

Next, return to or reactivate Word and, if the document you want to print is not in memory, either click the 'Open' button on the Toolbar, or use the **File, Open** command, to display the Open dialogue box shown overleaf.

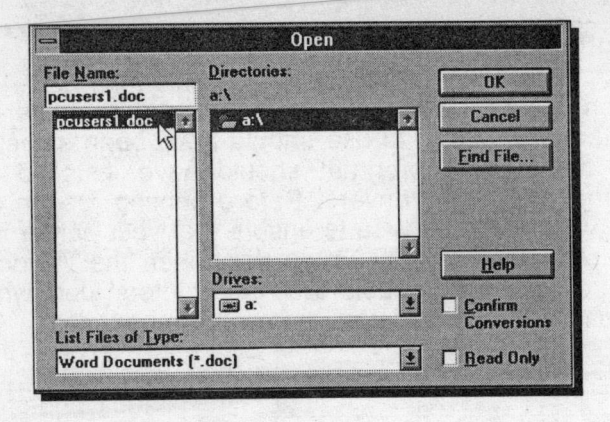

Use this dialogue box to locate the file (document) you want to print, which will be found on the drive and directory on which you saved it originally. Select it and click the **OK** button (or double-click its name), to load it into your computer's memory.

To print your document, do one of the following:

- Click the Print icon on the Toolbar, shown here, which prints the document using the current defaults.

- Use the **File, Print** command which opens the 'Print' box, shown below.

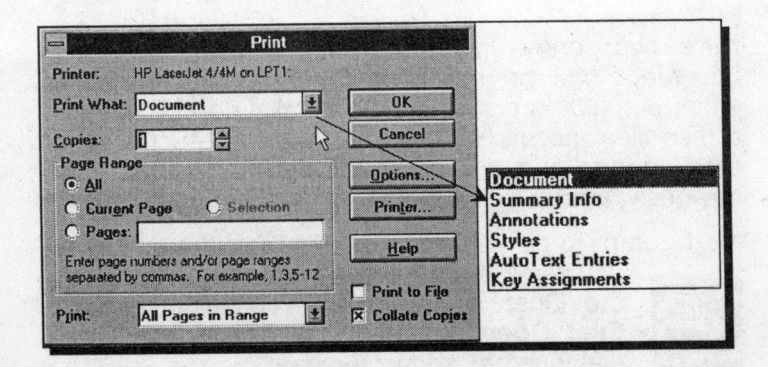

The settings in the Print dialogue box allow you to select the number of copies, and which pages, you want printed. You can also select to print the document, the summary information relating to that document, annotations, styles, etc., as shown in the drop-down list also on the previous page.

You can even change the selected printer by clicking the **Printer** button which displays the following dialogue box.

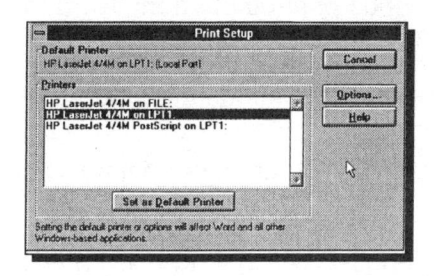

From this dialogue box you can select the default printer or any other installed printer. Clicking the **Options** button, displays the Setup dialogue box, shown below, which allows you to select the paper size, orientation needed, printer resolution, etc.

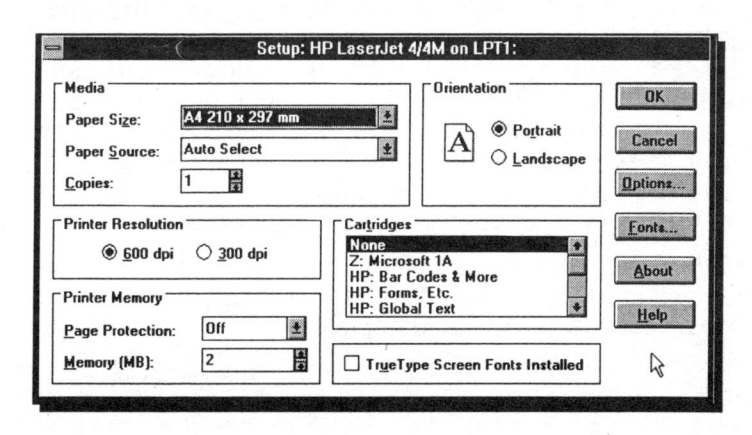

The **Options** button of the Setup dialogue box allows selection of graphics mode, graphics quality, and halftone options.

The **Options** button on the Print dialogue box, on the other hand, gives you access to some more advanced print options, such as printing in reverse order, or with and without annotations, hidden text, field codes or document summary information.

Clicking the **OK** button on these various multi-level dialogue boxes, causes Word to accept your selections and return you to the previous level dialogue box, until the Print dialogue box is reached. Selecting **OK** on this first level dialogue box, sends print output from Word to your selection, either the printer connected to your computer, or to an encoded file on disc. Selecting **Cancel** on any level dialogue box, aborts the selections made at that level.

Do remember that, whenever you change printers, the appearance of your document may change, as Word uses the fonts available with the newly selected printer. This can affect the line lengths, which in turn will affect both the tabulation and pagination of your document.

Before printing to paper, click the Print Preview icon on the Toolbar, shown here, or use the **File, Print Preview** command, to see how much of your document will fit on your selected page size. This depends very much on the chosen font. Thus, the **Print Preview** option allows you to see the layout of the final printed page, which can save a few trees and equally important to you, a lot of frustration and wear and tear on your printer.

Other enhancements of your document, such as selection of fonts, formatting of text, and pagination, will be discussed in the next chapter.

5. FORMATTING WORD DOCUMENTS

Formatting involves the appearance of individual words or even characters, the line spacing and alignment of paragraphs, and the overall page layout of the entire document. These functions are carried out in Word in several different ways.

Primary page layout and text formatting can be included in Style Sheets and Templates. Within any document, however, you can override Paragraph Style formats by applying text formatting and enhancements manually to selected text. To cancel manual formatting, select the text and use the

Edit, Undo Formatting

command, or (<Ctrl+Z>). The selected text reverts to its original format.

Formatting Text

The fonts available in Word depend on the printer(s) you have set-up in Microsoft Windows and selected in Word with the

File, Print, Printer

command. With Windows you can have fonts that display on your screen but that your printer cannot print, and vice versa.

If you select a printer font for which there is no exact screen font, then Word will select the nearest available to display your work. Similarly, if the font selected is not available to your printer, Word will select the nearest available and will use that when printing. You might choose to do the latter, because you plan to print on a different printer from the one attached to your system. When you open your document on the computer that has the specified font, Word will display and print your document with the correct font.

Originally, the title of the memo **pcusers1**, was typed in the 14 point size Arial typeface, while the subtitle and the main text were typed in 12 and 10 point size Times New Roman, respectively.

To change this memo into what appears on the screen dump displayed below, first select the title of the memo and format it to bold, italics, 18 point size Arial and centre it between the margins, then select the subtitle and format it to bold, 14 point size Times New Roman.

Finally select each paragraph of the main body of the memo in turn, and format it to 12 point size Times New Roman. All of this formatting can be achieved by using the buttons on the Formatting bar shown below (see also the section entitled 'Paragraph Alignment').

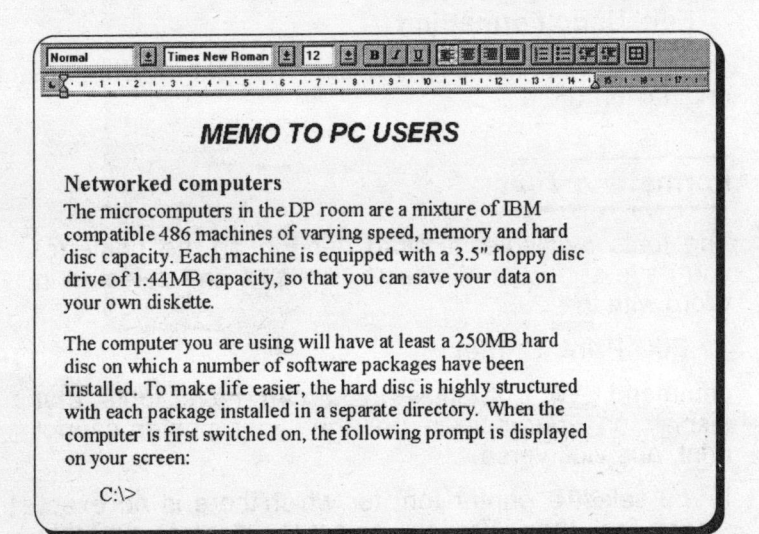

MEMO TO PC USERS

Networked computers

The microcomputers in the DP room are a mixture of IBM compatible 486 machines of varying speed, memory and hard disc capacity. Each machine is equipped with a 3.5" floppy disc drive of 1.44MB capacity, so that you can save your data on your own diskette.

The computer you are using will have at least a 250MB hard disc on which a number of software packages have been installed. To make life easier, the hard disc is highly structured with each package installed in a separate directory. When the computer is first switched on, the following prompt is displayed on your screen:

C:\>

If you can't access these font styles, it will probably be because your printer does not support them, in which case you will need to select other fonts that are supported.

Save the result under the new filename **pcusers2** - use the **File, Save As** command.

In Word all manual formatting, including the selection of font, point size, style (bold, italic, strike-through, hidden and capitals), colour, super/subscript, and various underlines, are carried out by first selecting the text and then executing the formatting command.

The easiest way of activating the formatting commands is from the Formatting toolbar. Another way is to use the

F_ormat, _Font

command, which displays the following dialogue box:

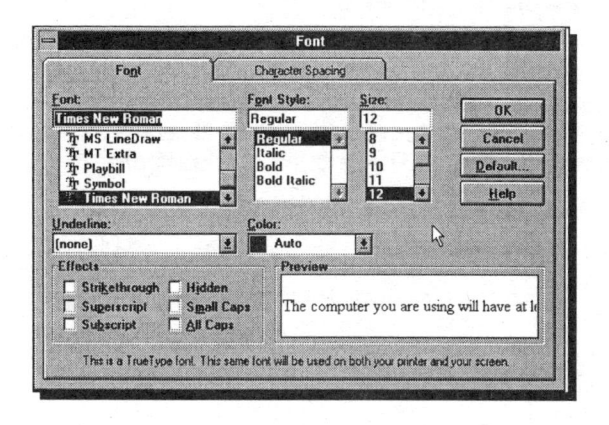

Yet another method is by using quick keys, some of which are listed below:

To Format	*Type*
Bold	Ctrl+B
Italic	Ctrl+I
Underline	Ctrl+U
Word underline	Ctrl+Shift+W
Double underline	Ctrl+Shift+D

There are quick keys to do almost anything, but the problem is remembering them! We find that those listed here are the most useful and the easiest to remember.

Text Enhancements

Word defines a paragraph, as any text which is followed by a paragraph mark, which is created by pressing the <Enter> key. So single line titles, as well as long typed text, can form paragraphs.

The paragraph symbol, shown here, is only visible if you have selected it from the Formatting bar.

Paragraph Alignment:

Word allows you to align a paragraph at the left margin (the default), at the right margin, centred between both margins, or justified between both margins. As with most operations there are several ways to perform alignment in Word. Three such methods are:

- Using buttons on the **Formatting bar**.
- Using keyboard short cuts, when available.
- Using the **Format**, **Paragraph** menu command.

The table below describes the buttons on the Formatting bar and their keystroke shortcuts.

Buttons on Formatting bar	Paragraph Alignment	Keystrokes
	Left	<Ctrl+L>
	Centre	<Ctrl+E>
	Right	<Ctrl+R>
	Justify	<Ctrl+J>

The display below shows the dialogue box resulting from using the **Format**, **Paragraph** command in which you can specify the **Left, Right**, or **Special** indentation required.

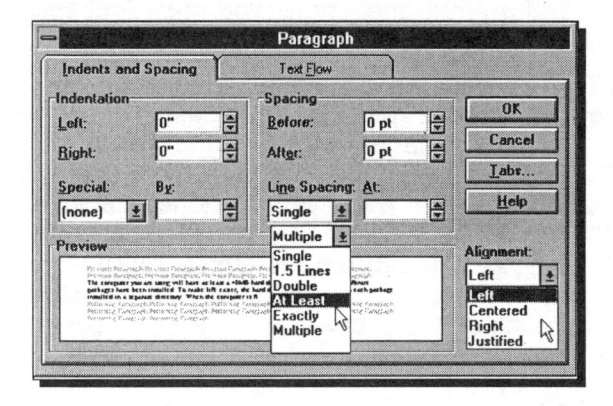

Paragraph Spacing:

The above Paragraph dialogue box can also be used to display a paragraph on screen, or print it on paper, in single-line, 1½-line, or double-line spacing. You can even set the spacing to any value you want by using the **At Least** option, as shown on the above screen dump, then specify what interval you want.

The available shortcut keys for paragraph spacing are as follows:

To Format	*Type*
Single-spaced lines	Ctrl+1
One-and-a-half-spaced lines	Ctrl+5
Double-spaced lines	Ctrl+2

Whichever of the above methods is used, formatting can take place either before or after the text is entered. If formatting is selected first, then text will type in the chosen format until a further formatting command is given. If, on the other hand, you choose to enter text and then format it afterwards, you must first select the text to be formatted, then activate the formatting.

Word gives you the choice of 4 units to work with, inches, centimetres, points or picas. These can be selected by using the **Tools**, **Options** command, choosing the **General** tab of the displayed Options dialogue box, and clicking the down arrow against the **Measurement Units** list box, shown open here, which is to be found at the bottom of the dialogue box.

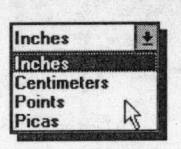

Indenting Text:

Most documents will require some form of paragraph indenting. An indent is the space between the margin and the edge of the text in the paragraph. When an indent is set (on the left or right side of the page), any justification on that side of the page sets at the indent, not the page border.

To illustrate indentation, open the file **pcusers2**, select the first paragraph, and then choose the **Format**, **Paragraph** command. In the **Indentation** field, select 0.5" for both **Left** and **Right**, as shown on the next page. On clicking **OK**, the first selected paragraph is displayed indented.

The **Indentation** option of the **Format**, **Paragraph** command, can be used to create 'hanging' indents, where all the lines in a paragraph, including any text on the first line that follows a tab, are indented by a specified amount. This is often used in lists to emphasise certain points.

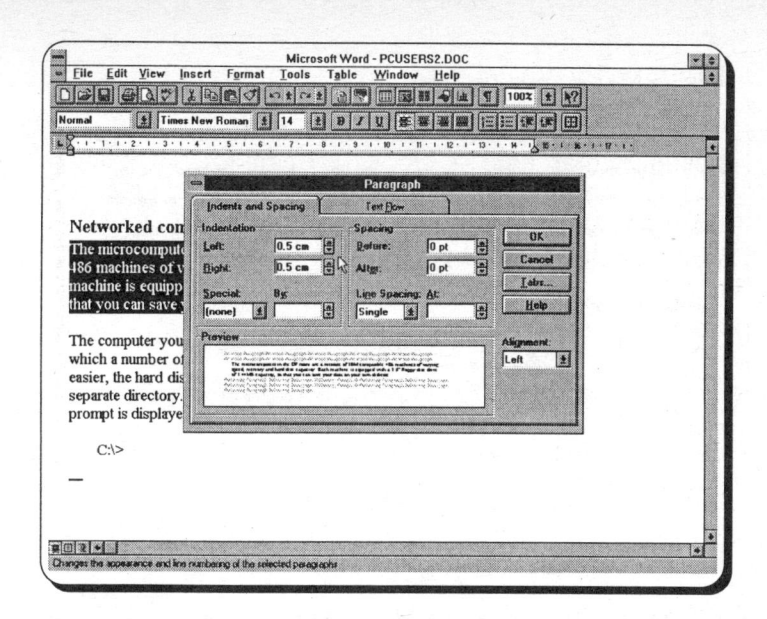

To illustrate the method, use the **pcusers1** file and add at the end of it, after the 'C:\>' prompt, the text shown overleaf, but please read on before doing so.

After you have typed the text in, save the enlarged memo as **pcusers3**, before going on with formatting the new information. This is done as a precaution in case anything goes wrong with the formatting - it is sometimes much easier to reload a saved file (using the **File, Open** command), than it is to try to unscramble a wrongly formatted document!

To find out what is on your hard disc, type

DIR   (and press the <Enter> key)

which will produce a list of all the filenames on the 'Root' directory (the one with the C:\> prompt) - directories are displayed with their names in angle brackets, for example <DOS>. If your hard disc is structured correctly, then the programs that make up a package would have been installed in a separate directory. For example:

Name Description

DOS Holds the operating system's commands that allow you to use your PC.

QB45 Holds the Microsoft Quick Basic version 4.5 suite of programs which allow you to write and compile fully structured Basic programs. It is one of the best versions of non-visual Basic available on the market.

Windows Holds the suite of programs that controls your Windows environment.

Next, highlight the last 4 paragraphs above, use the **Fo̱rmat**, **P̱aragraph** command, and select 'Hanging' under **Special** and 2.5 cm under **By̱**. On clicking the **OK** button, the text formats as shown, but it is still highlighted. To remove the highlighting, click the mouse button anywhere on the page. The second and following lines of the third paragraph selected, should be indented 2.5 cm from the left margin.

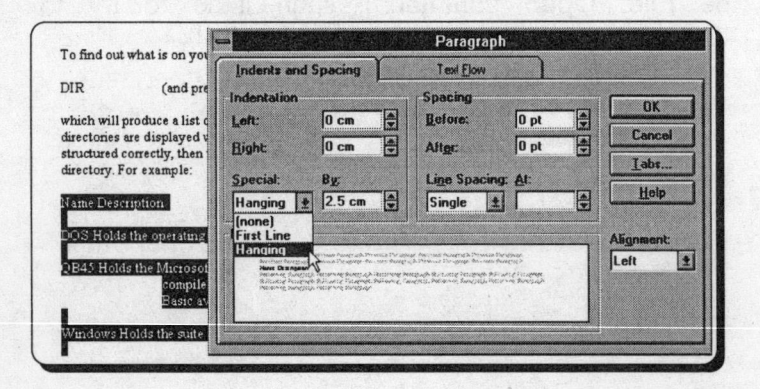

This is still not very inspiring, so to complete the effect we will edit the first lines of each paragraph as follows:

Place the cursor in front of the word 'Description' in paragraph 4 and press the <Tab> key once. This places the start of the word in the same column as the indented text of the third paragraph. To complete the effect place tabs before the word 'Holds' in the next three paragraphs, until your hanging indents are correct, as shown below.

To find out what is on your hard disc, type

DIR   (and press the <Enter> key)

which will produce a list of all the filenames on the 'Root' directory (the one with the C:\> prompt) - directories are displayed with their names in angle brackets, for example <DOS>. If your hard disc is structured correctly, then the programs that make up a package would have been installed in a separate directory. For example:

Name   Description

DOS   Holds the operating system's commands that allow you to use your PC.

QB45   Holds the Microsoft Quick Basic version 4.5 suite of programs which
            allow you to write and compile fully structured Basic programs. It is one
            of the best versions of non-visual Basic available on the market.

Windows   Holds the suite of programs that controls your Windows environment.

This may seem like a complicated rigmarole to go through each time you want the hanging indent effect, but with Word you will eventually set up all your indents, etc., in templates. Then all you do is click in a paragraph to produce them.

When you finish formatting the document, save it under its current filename either with the **F**ile, **S**ave command (<Ctrl+S>), or by clicking the Save button. This command does not display a dialogue box, so you use it when you do not need to make any changes to the saving operation.

Inserting Bullets:

Bullets are small characters you can insert, anywhere you like, in the text of your document to improve visual impact. In Word there are several choices for displaying lists with bullets or numbers. As well as the two Formatting bar buttons, others are made available through the

F_ormat, Bullets and _Numbering

command, which displays the following dialogue box:

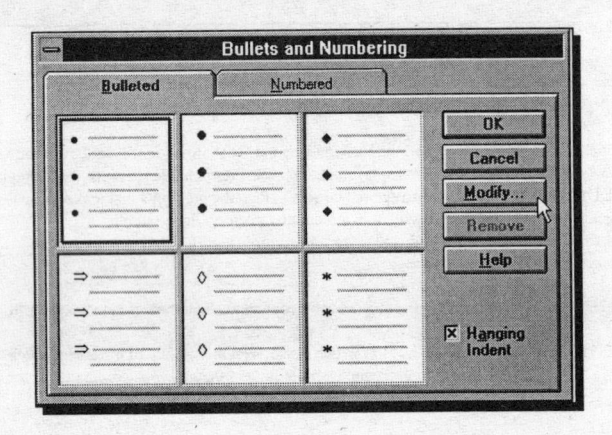

You can select any of the bullets shown here, or you could click the **Modify** button to change the size of the bullet, or the indentation.

Further, by pressing the **Bullet** button on the Modify Bulleted List dialogue box which would be displayed, you could select any character from the Symbol typeface or other available type-faces.

If you select the **Numbered** tab, a similar dialogue box is displayed, giving you a choice of several numbering systems and the ability to modify them.

Once inserted, you can copy, move or cut a bulleted line in the same way as any other text. However, you can not delete a bullet with the <BkSp> or <Del> keys.

Formatting with Page Tabs

You can format text in columns by using tab stops. Word has default left tab stops every 1.27 cm from the left margin, as shown here. This symbol appears on the left edge of the ruler (see below).

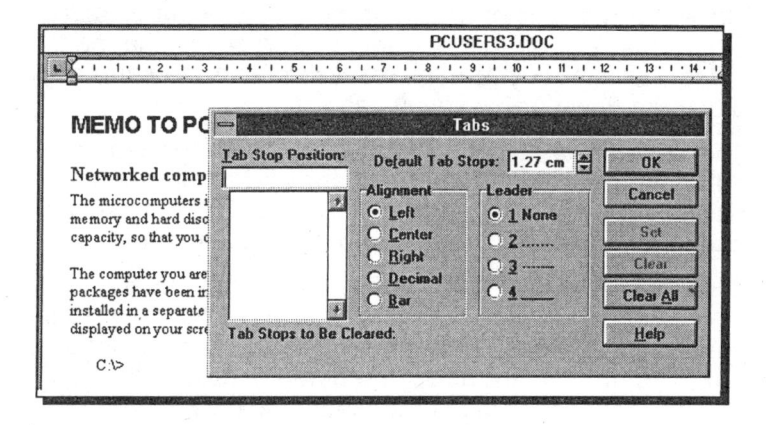

To set tabs, use either the **Format**, **Tabs** command which produces the Tab dialogue box, or click on the tab symbol on the left of the Ruler which rotates through the available tab stops.

The tab stop types available have the following function:

Button	Name	Effect
	Left	Left aligns text after the tab stop.
	Centre	Centres text on tab stop.
	Right	Right aligns text after the tab stop.
	Decimal	Aligns decimal point with tab stop.

To clear the ruler of tab settings press the **Clear All** button on the Tabs dialogue box. When you set a tab stop on the ruler, all default tab stops to the left of the one you are setting are removed. In addition, tab stops apply either to the paragraph containing the cursor, or to any selected paragraphs.

As all paragraph formatting, such as tab stops, is placed at the end of a paragraph, if you want to carry the formatting of the current paragraph to the next, press <Enter>. If you don't want formatting to carry on, press the down arrow key instead.

The easiest way to set a tab is to click on the tab type button you want and then point and click at the required position on the lower half of the ruler. To remove an added tab, point to it, click and drag it off the ruler.

If you want tabular text to be separated by characters instead of by spaces, select one of the three available characters from the **Leader** box in the Tabs dialogue box. The options are none (the default), dotted, dashed, or underline. The Contents and Index pages of this book are set with right tabs and dotted leader characters.

Formatting with Styles

We saw earlier in Chapter 5, how you can format your work using Paragraph Styles, but we confined ourselves to using the default **Normal** style only. In this section we will get to grips with how to create, modify, use, and manage styles.

As mentioned previously, a Paragraph Style is a set of formatting instructions which you save so that you can use it repeatedly within a document or in different documents. A collection of Paragraph Styles forms a Style Sheet which could be deemed appropriate for, say, all your memos, so it can be used to preserve uniformity. It maintains consistency and saves time by not having to format each paragraph individually.

Further, should you decide to change a style, all the paragraphs associated with that style reformat automatically. Finally, if you want to provide a pattern for shaping a final document, then you use what is known as a Template. All documents which have not been assigned a document template, use the **Normal.dot** template, by default.

Paragraph Styles:

Paragraph Styles contain paragraph and character formats and a name can be attached to these formatting instructions. From then on, applying the style name is the same as formatting that paragraph with the same instructions.

You can create a style by example, either with the use of the Formatting bar or the keyboard, or you can create a style from scratch, before you use it, by selecting the **Format, Style** menu command. By far the simplest way of creating a style is by example.

Creating Paragraph Styles by Example: Previously, we spent some time manually creating some hanging indents in the last few paragraphs of the **pcusers3** document. To create a style from this previous work, place the insertion pointer in one of these paragraphs, say, in the 'Name Description' line, and highlight the entire name of the existing style in the Formatting bar's Style box, as shown below.

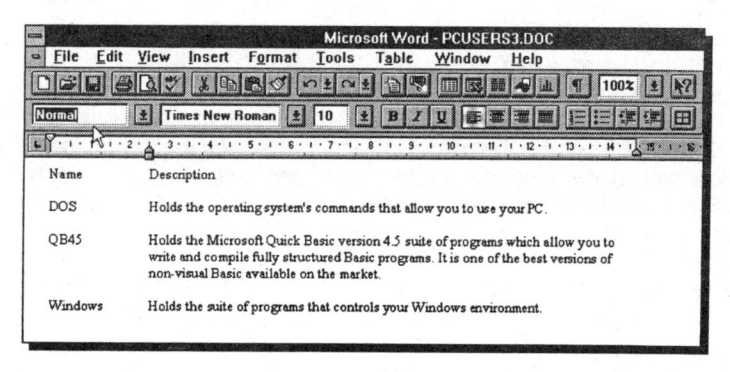

Name	Description
DOS	Holds the operating system's commands that allow you to use your PC.
QB45	Holds the Microsoft Quick Basic version 4.5 suite of programs which allow you to write and compile fully structured Basic programs. It is one of the best versions of non-visual Basic available on the market.
Windows	Holds the suite of programs that controls your Windows environment.

Then, type the new style name you want to create, say, 'Hanging Indent', and press <Enter>.

Finally, highlight the last three paragraphs with hanging indents and change their style to the new 'Hanging Indent', by clicking the mouse in the Style box button and selecting the appropriate style from the displayed list, as shown below.

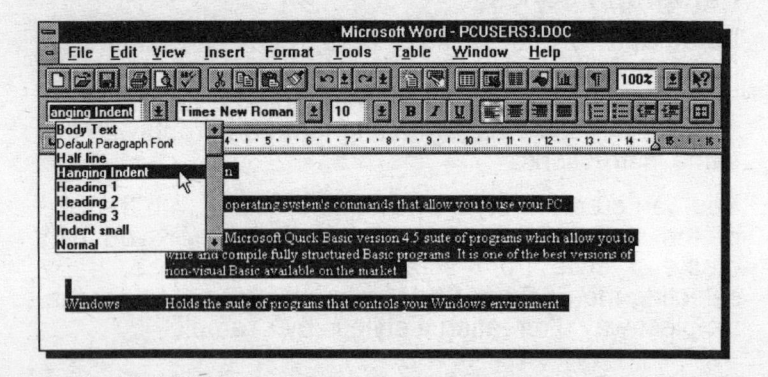

Creating Styles with the Menu Command: You can create, or change, a style before you apply any formatting to a paragraph, by using the **Format**, **Style** command. This displays the Style dialogue box, in which you can choose which style you want to change from the displayed **Styles** list.

Having selected the style you want to change (or not, as the case may be), click the **Modify** button which produces the Modify Style dialogue box. From here you can create a new style, or modify an existing style, by changing the formatting of characters, borders, paragraphs, and tab stops. You can even select which style should follow your current style.

If you have a lot of changes to make to a style, or you are creating your own personal style sheet, then it might be better if you created a template instead.

Document Templates:

A document template provides the overall pattern of your final document. It can contain:

- Paragraph styles and style sheets, which can control your paragraph and page set-up.
- Boilerplate text, which is text that remains the same in every document.
- AutoText (Glossary in previous versions), which is standard text and graphics that you could insert in a document by typing the name of the AutoText entry.
- Macros, which are programs that can change the menus and key assignments to comply with the type of document you are creating.

If you don't assign a template to a document, then the default **Normal.dot** template is used by Word. To create a new document template, you either modify an existing one, create one from scratch, or create one based on the formatting of an existing document.

To illustrate this last point, we will create a simple document template, which we will call **Pcuser**, based on the formatting of the **pcusers3** document. But first, make sure you have defined the 'Hanging Indent' style as explained earlier, and that the file is opened. Then select the **File, New** command which displays the New dialogue box, shown here.

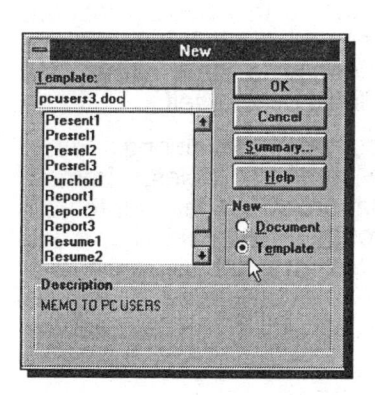

Next, select **Template** in the **New** field box, type in the **Template** box the name of the document (and its extension) on which you want the new template to be based, and click **OK**.

Finally, choose the **File, Save As** command, type the template name (**Pcuser** in this case), and click the **OK** button.

To use the new template, use the **File**, **New** command which causes the New dialogue box to be displayed. Select the name of the Template you want to use, from the **Template** list, as shown here, and click the **OK** button.

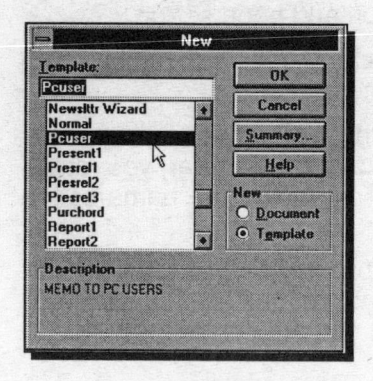

Templates can also contain Macros as well as AutoText; macros allow you to automate Word keystroke actions only, while AutoText speeds up the addition of boilerplate text and graphics into your document, however, these features are beyond the scope of this book.

* * *

Word has many more features, far too numerous to mention in the space allocated to this book. What we have tried to do is give you enough basic information so that you can have the confidence to forge ahead and explore the rest of its capabilities by yourself.

Perhaps, you might consider exploring page numbering, headers and footers, tables, frames, drawing, and outlining, in that order. We leave it to you. However, if you would prefer to be guided through these topics, then may we suggest you look up the later chapters of the book *Word 6 for Windows Explained* (BP354), also published by BERNARD BABANI (publishing) Ltd.

6. THE EXCEL SPREADSHEET

Microsoft Excel is a powerful and versatile software package which, over the last few years, has proved its usefulness, not only in the business world, but with scientific and engineering users as well.

The program's power lies in its ability to emulate everything that can be done by the use of pencil, paper and a calculator. Thus, it is an 'electronic spreadsheet' or simply a 'spreadsheet', a name which is also used to describe it and other similar products. Its power is derived from the power of the computer it is running on, and the flexibility and accuracy with which it can deal with the solution of the various applications it is programmed to manage. These can vary from budgeting and forecasting to the solution of complex scientific and engineering problems.

Starting the Excel Program

To start Excel, start Windows, open the Windows Program Manager, and if you are using a mouse, point to the Microsoft Excel icon, shown here, and double-click the left mouse button.

With the keyboard, after opening the Windows Program Manager, use the <Ctrl+Tab> key combination, until the Microsoft Office Group is highlighted, then use the cursor keys to highlight the Microsoft Excel application icon, and press the <Enter> key.

When Excel is loaded, a 'blank' spreadsheet screen displays with similar Title bar, Menu bar, Toolbar and Formatting bar to those of Word. Obviously there are some differences, but that is to be expected as the two programs serve different purposes.

The Excel Screen

The opening screen of Excel is shown below. It is perhaps worth looking at the various parts that make up this screen, or window, if only to see how similar it is to that of Word. Excel follows the usual Microsoft Windows conventions with which you should be very familiar by now.

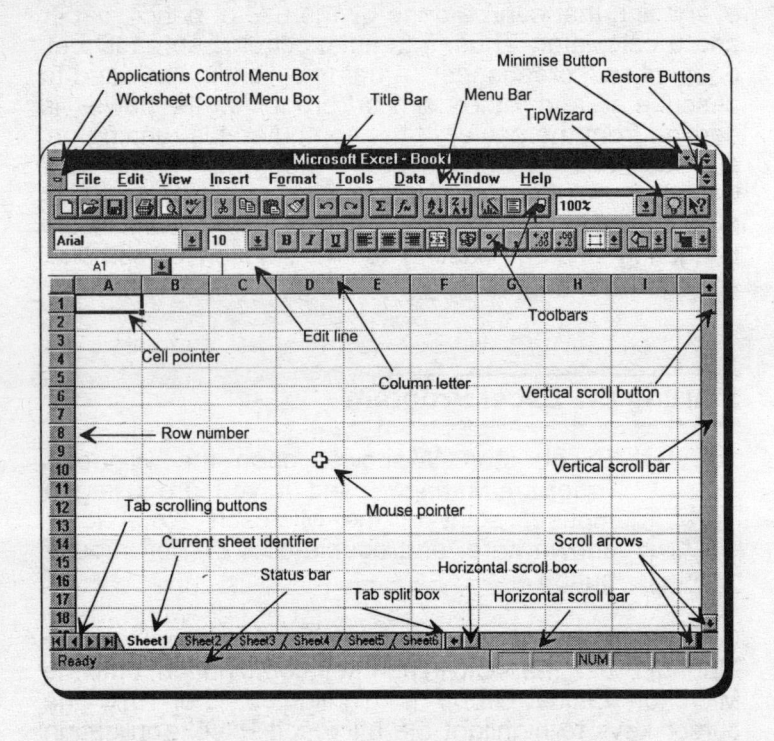

The window as shown takes up the full screen area available. If you click on the application restore button, the top one of the two restore buttons at the top right of the screen, you can make Excel show in a smaller window. This can be useful when you are running several applications at the same time and you want to transfer between them with the mouse.

Note that the Excel window, which in this case displays an empty and untitled book (Book1), has some areas which have identical functions to those of Word (refer to 'The Word Screen' section in Chapter 2), and other areas which have different functions. Below, we describe only the areas that are exclusive to Excel.

Area	*Function*
TipWizard	The bulb icon which lights up if there is a quicker or more efficient way of performing the action you have just performed. Clicking on the icon displays the tip, while clicking on the icon once more removes it.
Edit line	Contains the selection indicator (cell co-ordinates), and the contents or edit line box (can include a number, a label, or the formula behind a displayed result).
Cell pointer	Marks the current cell.
Column letter	The letter that identifies each column.
Row number	The number that identifies each row.
Tab scrolling	Clicking on these buttons, scrolls sheet tabs right or left, when there are more tabs than can be displayed at once.
Current sheet	Shows the current sheet amongst a number of sheets in a file. These are named Sheet1, Sheet2, Sheet3, and so on, by default, but can be changed to, say, North, South, East, and West. Clicking on a sheet tab, moves you to that sheet.

Tab split box   The split box which you drag left to see more of the scroll bar, or right to see more tabs.

There are two extra split boxes on Excel's worksheet screen dump, which have not been identified. Both of these have to do with splitting the screen; one horizontally (the split box for this is located at the extreme right of the screen above the 'top vertical scroll arrow' button), the other vertically (the split box for this is located at the extreme bottom-right corner of the screen, to the left of the 'right horizontal scroll arrow' button). The use of both these split boxes will be discussed later.

Getting Familiar with Excel

Excel has two options under the **H**elp menu which allow you to familiarise yourself with the package; **Q**uick Preview and **E**xamples and Demos.

The first one of these, is an interactive tutorial on four main options: Getting Started, What is New, Getting Information While You Work, and For Lotus 1-2-3 Users. To access this option, start Excel, then use the **H**elp, **Q**uick Preview command. This tutorial is a good introduction to the powerful features of Excel. It takes about half an hour to work through and is well worth the time. You can of course run through the different options as often as you like, and not necessarily in the presentation order. When you have finished, press the **R**eturn to Microsoft Excel button.

The second familiarisation option offers detailed information on a number of selected topics, and has the added ability of letting you practise on them. To access this option, start Excel and use the **H**elp, **E**xamples **and Demos** command, which causes the following screen to be displayed.

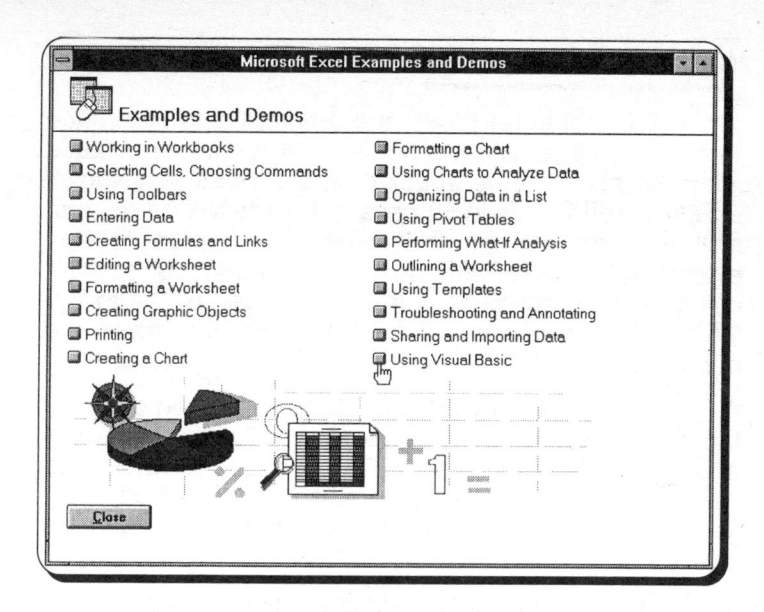

```
┌─────────────────────────────────────────────────────┐
│ —           Microsoft Excel Examples and Demos    ▼▲│
├─────────────────────────────────────────────────────┤
│   📖  Examples and Demos                            │
│                                                     │
│   ▣ Working in Workbooks        ▣ Formatting a Chart│
│   ▣ Selecting Cells, Choosing Commands              │
│                                 ▣ Using Charts to Analyze Data
│   ▣ Using Toolbars              ▣ Organizing Data in a List
│   ▣ Entering Data               ▣ Using Pivot Tables│
│   ▣ Creating Formulas and Links ▣ Performing What-If Analysis
│   ▣ Editing a Worksheet         ▣ Outlining a Worksheet
│   ▣ Formatting a Worksheet      ▣ Using Templates   │
│   ▣ Creating Graphic Objects    ▣ Troubleshooting and Annotating
│   ▣ Printing                    ▣ Sharing and Importing Data
│   ▣ Creating a Chart            ▣ Using Visual Basic│
│                                                     │
│   [ Close ]                                         │
└─────────────────────────────────────────────────────┘
```

As you can see from the list above, this option gives you far more detailed information on a much larger selection of topics. We suggest you return to this option often to complete your knowledge of the package.

Using Help in Excel

The Microsoft Excel Help Program provides a comprehensive on-line help in exactly the same way as the Microsoft Word Help program. No matter what you are doing, you can either press the **F1** function key to display context sensitive help screens, or click the Help button on the Standard toolbar, then move the modified mouse pointer to an area of the worksheet or on to a particular toolbar button and press the left mouse button, or choose **Help** from the Main Menu bar, to display a short menu, then choose **Index** to display the Excel Help index.

Worksheet Navigation

When you first enter Excel, the program sets up a huge electronic page, or worksheet, in your computer's memory, many times larger than the small part shown on the screen. Individual cells are identified by column and row location (in that order), with present size extending to 256 columns and 16,384 rows. The columns are labelled from A to Z, followed by AA to AZ, BA to BZ, and so on, to IV, while the rows are numbered from 1 to 16,384.

A worksheet can be thought of as a two-dimensional table made up of rows and columns. The point where a row and column intersect is called a cell, while the reference points of a cell are known as the cell address. The active cell (A1 when you first enter the program) is boxed.

Navigation around the worksheet is achieved by use of the four arrow keys (→↓←↑). Each time one of these keys is pressed, the active cell moves one position right, down, left or up, depending on which arrow key was pressed. The <PgDn> and <PgUp> keys can also be used to move down or up one visible page, respectively, while the <Ctrl+→> and <Ctrl+↓> key combinations can be used to move to the extreme right of the worksheet (column IV) or extreme bottom of the worksheet (row 16,384), respectively. Pressing the <Home> key, moves the active cell to the beginning of a row, while pressing the <Ctrl+Home> key combination moves the active cell to the home position, A1. Finally, the key combination <End+Home> can be used to move to the lower right corner of the worksheet's active area.

You can move the active cell with a mouse by pointing to the cell you want to activate and clicking the left mouse button. If the cell is not visible, move the window by clicking on the scroll bar arrowhead that points in the direction you want to move, or press the **F5** function key and specify the required cell address.

To move a page at a time, click in the scroll bar itself, or for larger moves, drag the box in the scroll bar (the furthest you can go with this method in an empty worksheet is cell location R54.

When you have finished navigating around the worksheet, press the <Ctrl+Home> key combination which will move the active cell to the A1 position (provided you have not fixed titles in any rows or columns or have no hidden rows or columns - more about these later). Note that the area within which you can move the active cell is referred to as the working area of the worksheet, while the letters and numbers in the border at the top and left of the working area give the 'co-ordinates' of the cells in a worksheet.

The location of the active cell is constantly monitored by the 'selection indicator' which is to be found on the extreme left below the lower Toolbar of the application window. As the active cell is moved, this indicator displays its address, as shown below. The contents of a cell are displayed above the column letters within what is known as the 'Edit line'. If you type text in the active cell, what you type appears in both the 'Edit line' and the cell itself. Typing a formula which is preceded by the equals sign (=) to, say, add the contents of three cells, causes the actual formula to appear in the 'Edit line', while the result of the actual calculation appears in the active cell when the <Enter> key is pressed.

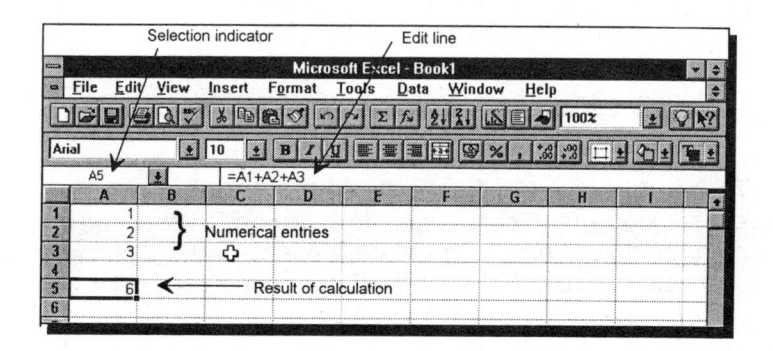

Moving Between Sheets:

You can scroll between sheets by clicking one of the arrows situated to the left of Sheet 1, as shown below. The inner arrows scroll sheets one at a time in the direction of the arrow, while the outer arrows scroll to the end, or beginning, of the group of available sheets. A sheet is then made current by clicking its tab.

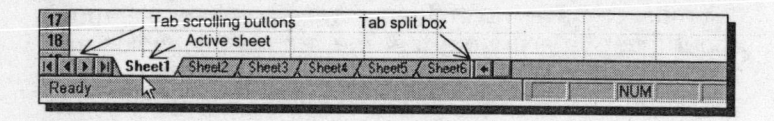

With the keyboard, you can scroll one sheet at a time, and make it active at the same time, by using the <Ctrl+PgDn> key combination. Using <Ctrl+PgUp> scrolls in the reverse direction.

To display more sheet tabs at a time, drag the split box to the right. The reverse action displays less sheet tabs. To rename sheets, double-click at their tab, then type a new name in the Rename Sheet dialogue box, as shown below.

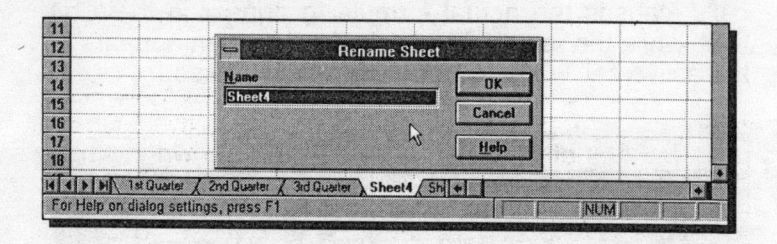

To insert a sheet in front of a certain sheet, make that sheet current, then use the **Insert, Worksheet** command sequence. To delete a sheet, make it current and use the **Edit, Delete Sheet** command sequence.

Rearranging Sheet Order:

If you need to rearrange the order in which sheets are being held in a workbook, you can do so by dragging a particular sheet to its new position, as shown below.

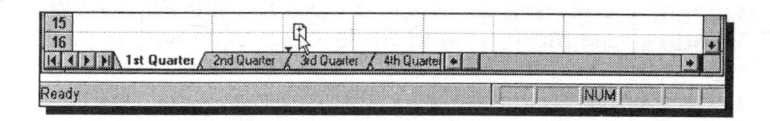

While you are dragging the tab of the sheet you want to move, the mouse pointer changes to an arrow pointing to a sheet. The small solid arrowhead to the left of the mouse pointer indicates the place where the sheet you are moving will be placed.

Grouping Worksheets:

You can select several sheets to group them together so that data entry, editing, or formatting can be made easier and more consistent.

To select adjacent sheets, click the first sheet tab, hold down the <Shift> key and then click the last sheet tab in the group. To select non-adjacent sheets, click the first sheet tab, hold down the <Ctrl> key and then click the other sheet tabs you want to group together.

Selecting sheets in the above manner, causes the word "[Group]" to appear in the Title bar of the active window, and the tabs of the selected sheets are shown in white. To cancel the selection, click at the tab of any sheet which is not part of the selected group.

Shortcut Menus:

While a range of cells in a sheet is selected, or a group of sheets is active, you can access a shortcut menu of relevant commands by pressing the right mouse button. This produces a shortcut menu of the most common commands relevant to what you are doing at the time.

Viewing Multiple Workbook Sheets

To see more clearly what you are doing when starting with multiple workbook sheets, type the text '1st' in location A1 of 1st Quarter sheet, '2nd' in the 2nd Quarter sheet, and so on. Then use the **Window, New Window** command to add three extra windows to your worksheet, and the **Window, Arrange, Tiled** command to display the four sheets as shown below.

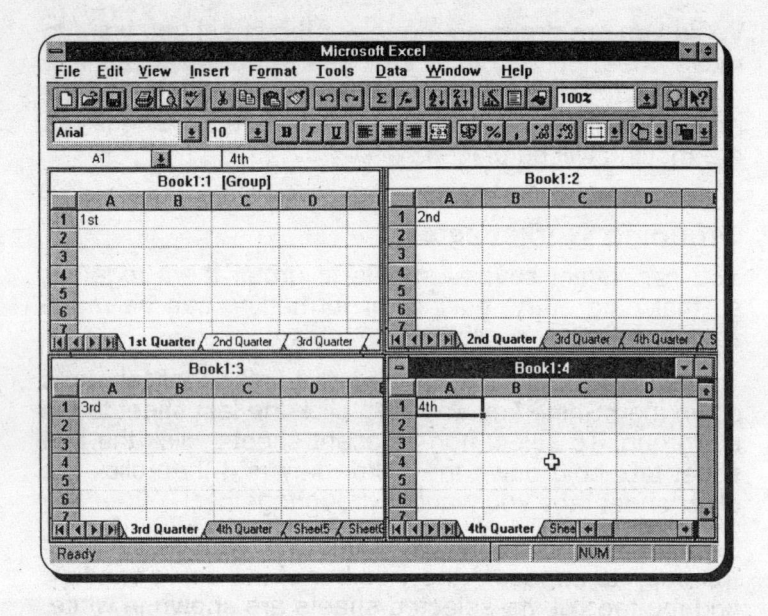

To move from one window to another, simply point with the mouse to the cell of the window you want to go to and click the left mouse button. To display a different sheet in each window, go to a window and click the sheet's tab.

To return to single-window view mode from a tiled mode, click the maximise button of the active window.

7. FILLING IN A WORKSHEET

Entering Information

We will now investigate how information can be entered into a worksheet. But first, make sure you are in Sheet1, then return to the Home (A1) position, by pressing the <Ctrl+Home> key combination, then type the words:

    PROJECT ANALYSIS

As you type, the characters appear in both the 'Edit line' and the active cell. If you make a mistake, press the <BkSp> key to erase the previous letter or the <Esc> key to start again. When you have finished, press <Enter>.

Note that what you have just typed in has been entered in cell A1, even though the whole of the word ANALYSIS appears to be in cell B1. If you use the right arrow key to move the active cell to B1 you will see that the cell is indeed empty.

Typing any letter at the beginning of an entry into a cell results in a 'text' entry being formed automatically, otherwise known as a 'label'. If the length of the text is longer than the width of a cell, it will continue into the next cell to the right of the current active cell, provided that cell is empty, otherwise the displayed information will be truncated.

To edit information already in a cell, double-click the cell in question, or make that cell the active cell and press the **F2** function key. The cursor keys, the <Home> and <End> keys, as well as the <Ins> and <Del> keys can be used to move the cursor and/or edit information as required.

You can also 'undo' the most recent operation that has been carried out since the program was last in the **Ready** mode, by using the **Edit, Undo Entry** command.

Next, use the arrow keys to move the active cell to B3 and type

    Jan

Pressing the right arrow key (→) will automatically enter the typed information into the cell and also move the active cell one cell to the right, in this case C3. Now type

    Feb

and press <Enter>.

The looks of a worksheet can be enhanced somewhat by using different types of borders around specific cells. To do this, first select the range of cells you would like to surround with a border, then click at the down arrow of the Borders icon on the second Toolbar, shown here, which displays a choice of twelve different types of borders, as shown below.

Selecting a Range of Cells:

To select a range of cells, say, A3:C3, point to cell A3, press the left mouse button, and while holding it pressed, drag the mouse to the right, as shown below.

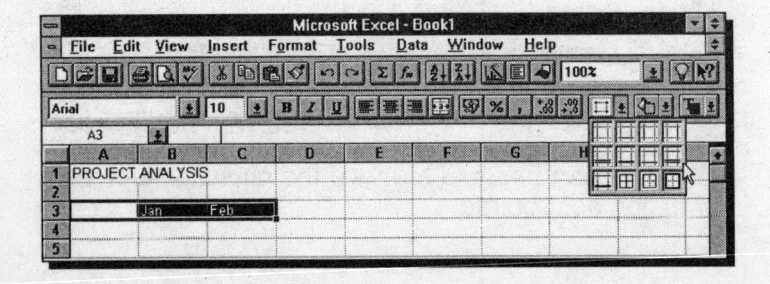

In our example, we have selected the cell range A3:C3, then we chose the 8th border from the display table. Moving the cell pointer to the right, out of the way reveals a better looking worksheet, as follows:

To select a range from the keyboard, first make active the first cell in the range, then hold down the <Shift> key and use the right arrow key (→) to highlight the required range.

To select a 3D range, across several sheets, select the range in the first sheet, release the mouse button, hold down the <Shift> key, and click the Tab of the last sheet in the range.

To continue with our example, move to cell A4 and type the label Income, then enter the numbers 14000 and 15000 in cells B4 and C4, respectively. What you should have on your screen now, is shown below.

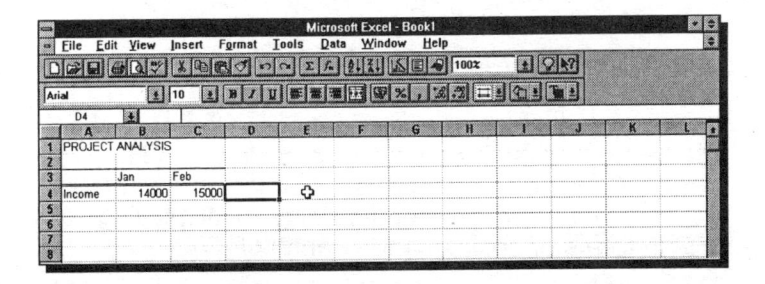

Note how the labels 'Jan' and 'Feb' do not appear above the numbers 14000 and 15000. This is because by default, labels are left justified, while numbers are right justified.

Changing Text Alignment and Fonts:

One way of improving the looks of this worksheet is to also right justify the text 'Jan' and 'Feb' within their respective cells. To do this, move the active cell to B3 and select the range B3 to C3 by dragging the mouse, then either click the 'Align Right' icon, shown here, or choose the

Format, **Cells**

command, then select the **Alignment** tab from the displayed Format Cells dialogue box, shown below, choose the **Right** button from the list under **Horizontal**, and press **OK**.

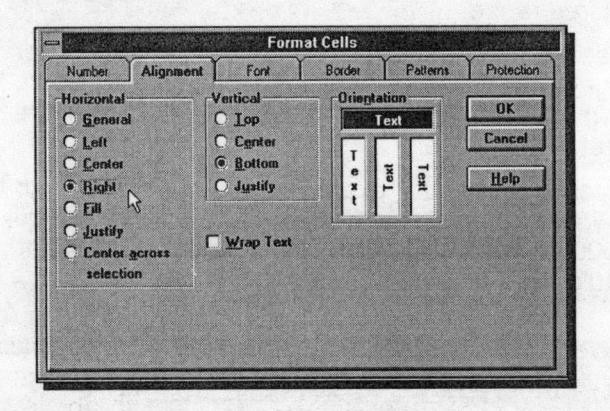

No matter which method you choose, the text should now appear right justified within their cells. However, although the latter method is lengthier, it nevertheless provides you with greater flexibility in displaying text, both in terms of position and orientation.

We could further improve the looks of our worksheet by choosing a different font for the heading 'Project Analysis'. To achieve this, select cell A1, then click on the 'Font Size' button on the second Toolbar, to reveal the band of available point sizes for the selected font, as shown overleaf. From this band, choose 14, then click in succession the 'Bold' and 'Italic' icons.

Finally, since the numbers in cells B4 to C4 represent money, it would be better if these were prefixed with the £ sign. To do this, select the cell range B4:C4, then either click the 'Currency Style' button on the second Toolbar, shown here, or choose the

F̲ormat, S̲tyle

command and select **Currency** from the list under **S̲tyle Name** in the displayed Style dialogue box.

The numbers within the chosen range will now be displayed in currency form, provided the width of the cells is sufficient to accommodate them. In our example, the entered numbers are far too long to fit in currency form in the default cell width and appear as shown under the 'Feb' entry.

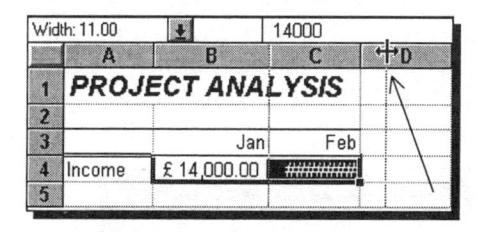

To see the actual numbers we must increase the width of the columns B4:C4 to 11 characters wide (as shown at the top left of the adjacent display). To do this, place the mouse pointer in between the column letters on the dividing line, and drag the pointer to the right, as pointed to above, until the width of the column is displayed as 11.00. The resultant worksheet should look as follows:

Saving a Worksheet

Now, let us assume that we would like to stop at this point, but would also like to save the work entered so far before leaving the program. First, return to the Home position by pressing <Ctrl+Home>. This is good practice because when a workbook is opened later, the position of the cell pointer at the time of saving the file appears at the top left corner of the opened worksheet which might cause confusion if below and to the right of it there are no entries - you might think that you opened an empty worksheet.

Next, choose the

File, Save

command to reveal the Save As dialogue box, select to save your work in the **a:** drive, and type the new name of the file, say, **project1** in the **File Name** box (the extension **.xls** is added by the program), which replaces the default highlighted name **book1.xls**.

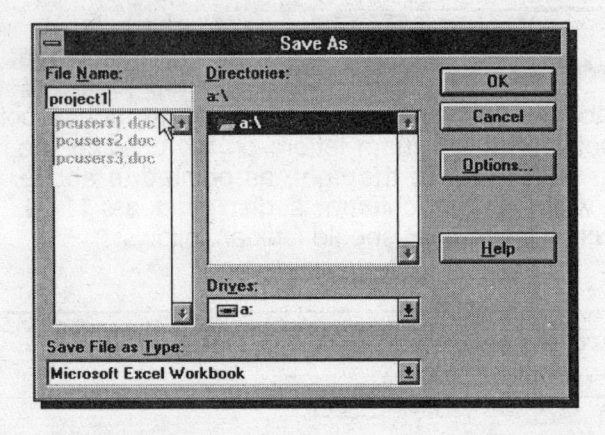

Clicking the **OK** button, causes the Summary Info dialogue box to appear on the screen. If you do not want to fill-in this dialogue box, click the **OK** button.

Opening a Worksheet

An already saved worksheet - a workbook - can be opened by either clicking at the 'Open' icon, shown here, or selecting the

File, Open

command which displays the Open dialogue box. Do not forget to change the drive to **a:**, if that is where you saved your work. Excel asks for a filename to open, with the default name ***.xl*** being displayed in the **File Name** box. If you haven't saved it, don't worry as you could just as easily start afresh.

Next use the **F2** function key to 'Edit' existing entries or simply retype the contents of cells (see below for formatting) so that your worksheet looks as follows:

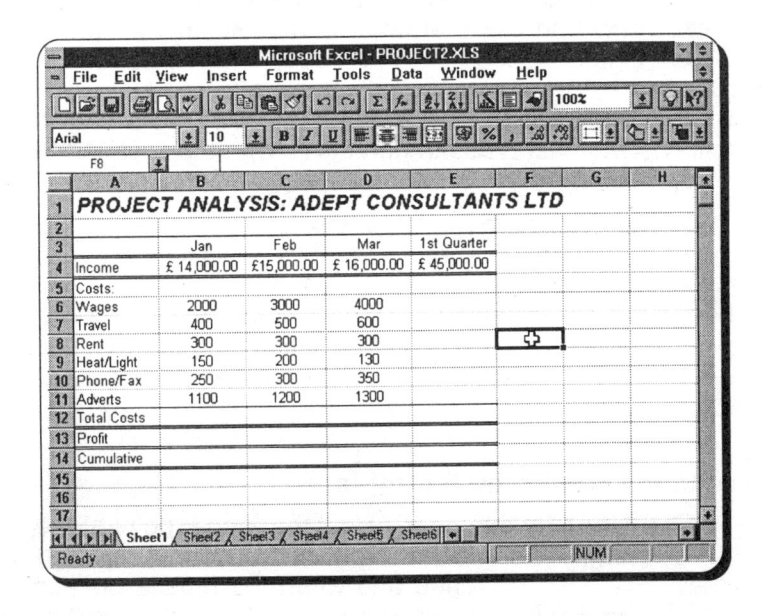

	A	B	C	D	E
1	PROJECT ANALYSIS: ADEPT CONSULTANTS LTD				
2					
3		Jan	Feb	Mar	1st Quarter
4	Income	£ 14,000.00	£15,000.00	£ 16,000.00	£ 45,000.00
5	Costs:				
6	Wages	2000	3000	4000	
7	Travel	400	500	600	
8	Rent	300	300	300	
9	Heat/Light	150	200	130	
10	Phone/Fax	250	300	350	
11	Adverts	1100	1200	1300	
12	Total Costs				
13	Profit				
14	Cumulative				

Formatting Entries

The information in cell A1 (PROJECT ANALYSIS: ADEPT CONSULTANTS LTD) was entered left justified and formatted by clicking on the 'Font Size' button on the second Toolbar, and selecting 14 point font size from the band of available font sizes, then clicking in succession the 'Bold' and 'Italic' icons.

The text in the cell block B3:E3 was formatted by first selecting the range and then clicking the 'Centre' alignment icon on the second Toolbar, so the text within the range is displayed centre justified.

The numbers within the cell block B4:E4 were formatted by first selecting the range, then clicking the 'Currency Style' icon on the second Toolbar, shown here, so the numbers appear with two digits after the decimal point and prefixed with the £ sign.

All the text appearing in column A (apart from that in cell A1) was just typed in (left justified), as shown in the screen dump on the previous page.

The lines, like the double line stretching from A3 to E3 were entered by first selecting the cell range A3:E3, then clicking the down-arrow of the 'Borders' icon on the second Toolbar, and selecting the appropriate border from the 12 displayed options.

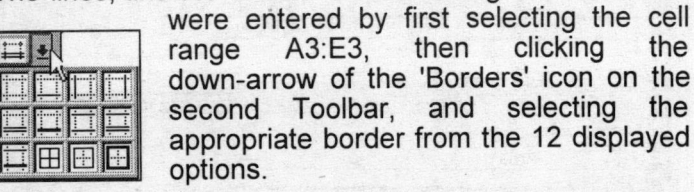

Filling a Range by Example:

To fill a range by example, select the range, point at the bottom right corner of the selected range and when the mouse pointer changes to a small cross, drag the mouse in the required direction.

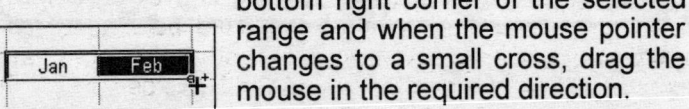

In the previous case, the next cell to the right will automatically fill with the text 'Mar' (Excel anticipates that you want to fill cells by example with the abbreviations for months, and does it for you). Not only that, but it also copies the format of the selected range forward. It is, therefore, evident that selecting ranges and using icons makes various tasks a lot easier.

Microsoft Excel allows you to format both text (labels) and numbers in any way you choose. For example, you can have numbers centre justified in their cells, if you so wished.

Entering Text, Numbers and Formulae:

When text, a number, a formula, or an Excel function is entered into a cell, or reference is made to the contents of a cell by the cell address, then the content of the status bar changes from **Ready** to **Enter**. This status can be changed back to **Ready** by either completing an entry and pressing <Enter> or one of the arrow keys, or by pressing <Esc>.

We can find the 1st quarter total income from consultancy, by activating cell E4, typing

   =B4+C4+D4

and pressing <Enter>. The total first quarter income is added, using the above formula, and the result is placed in cell E4.

Now complete the insertion into the spreadsheet of the various amounts under 'costs' and then choose the

   File, Save As

command to save the resultant worksheet under the filename **project2**, before going on any further. Remember that saving your work on disc often enough is a good thing to get used to, as even the shortest power cut can cause the loss of hours of hard work! Also remember that filenames should be limited to 8 alphanumeric characters, and must not contain any spaces. The extension **.xls** is added by Excel.

Using Functions

In our example, writing a formula that adds the contents of three columns is not too difficult or lengthy a task. But imagine having to add 20 columns! For this reason Excel has an in-built summation function which can be used to add any number of columns (or rows).

To illustrate how this and other functions can be used, activate cell E4 and press the Function Wizard button shown here. If the function you require appears on the displayed dialogue box under **Function Name**, choose it, otherwise select the appropriate class from the list under **Function Category**.

Choosing the **sum** function, inserts the entry SUM(number1,number2,...) in the Edit line. Clicking the **Next** button, causes the appearance of a second dialogue box, as shown in the composite screen dump below, which allows you to insert the range over which the function is to be effective.

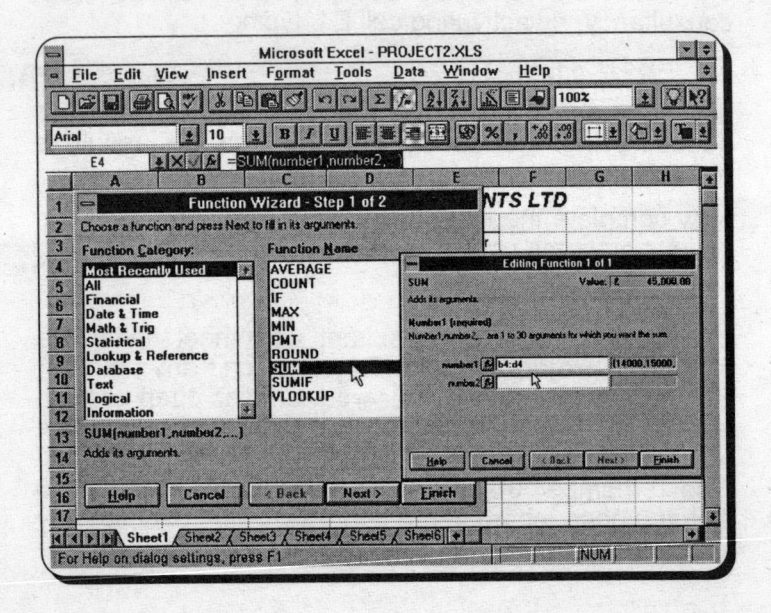

In this case, we enter B4:D4 as the range we want to summate is continuous. If the range is not continuous, separate the various continuous portions of it with a comma (,).

Pressing <Enter> or clicking the **Finish** button causes the result of the calculation to appear in the active cell.

Using the AutoSum Icon:

With addition, there is a better and quicker way of letting Excel work out the desired result. To illustrate this, select the cell range B6:E12, which contains the 'Costs' we would like to add up. To add these in both the horizontal and vertical direction, we include in the selected range an empty column to the right of the numbers and an empty row below the numbers, as shown below.

Pressing the 'AutoSum' icon, shown here, inserts the result of the summations in the empty column and row, as shown below. The selected range remains selected so that any other formatting can be applied by simply pressing the appropriate icon button.

Now complete the insertion of formulae in the rest of the worksheet, noting that 'Profit', in B13, is the difference between 'Income' and 'Total Cost', calculated by the formula **=B4-B12**. To complete the entry, this formula should be copied using the 'fill by example' method into the three cells to its right.

The 'Cumulative' entry in cell B14 should be a simple reference to cell B13, that is **=B13**, while in cell C14 should be **=B14+C13**. Similarly, the latter formula is copied into cell D14 using the 'fill by example' method.

Finally, format the entire range B6:E12 as currency by selecting the range and clicking the 'Currency Style' button.

If you make any mistakes and copy formats or information into cells you did not mean to, use the

Edit, Undo

command which allows you to selectively undo what you were just doing. To blank the contents within a range of cells, first select the range, then press the <Del> key.

The worksheet, up to this point, should look as follows:

	A	B	C	D	E	F	G	H
1	*PROJECT ANALYSIS: ADEPT CONSULTANTS LTD*							
2								
3		Jan	Feb	Mar	1st Quarter			
4	Income	£ 14,000.00	£15,000.00	£ 16,000.00	£ 45,000.00			
5	Costs:							
6	Wages	£ 2,000.00	£ 3,000.00	£ 4,000.00	£ 9,000.00			
7	Travel	£ 400.00	£ 500.00	£ 600.00	£ 1,500.00			
8	Rent	£ 300.00	£ 300.00	£ 300.00	£ 900.00			
9	Heat/Light	£ 150.00	£ 200.00	£ 130.00	£ 480.00			
10	Phone/Fax	£ 250.00	£ 300.00	£ 350.00	£ 900.00			
11	Adverts	£ 1,100.00	£ 1,200.00	£ 1,300.00	£ 3,600.00			
12	Total Costs	£ 4,200.00	£ 5,500.00	£ 6,680.00	£ 16,380.00			
13	Profit	£ 9,800.00	£ 9,500.00	£ 9,320.00	£ 28,620.00			
14	Cumulative	£ 9,800.00	£19,300.00	£ 28,620.00				
15								

If everything is correct, use the **File, Save As** command to save the worksheet under the filename **project3**.

Printing a Worksheet

To print a worksheet, make sure that the printer you propose to use was defined when you first installed Windows.

If you have named more than one printer in your original installation of Windows, and want to select a printer other than your original first choice, then select the **File, Print** command and select the **Printer Setup** button on the displayed Print dialogue box.

The two dialogue boxes are shown below in a composite screen dump.

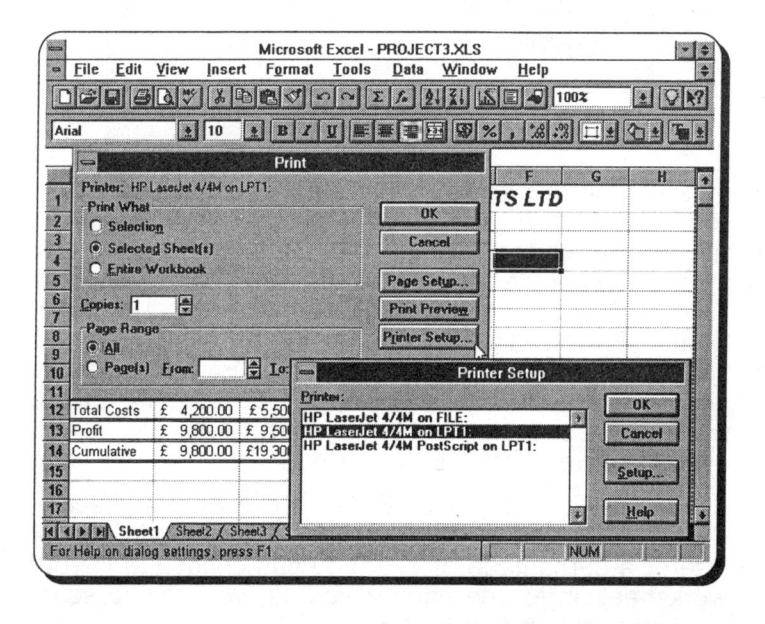

If you want to change the paper size, number of copies, print orientation, or printer resolution, choose the **Setup** button on the Printer Setup dialogue box which causes the printer specific Setup dialogue box to be displayed. The procedure is the same as in Microsoft Word.

You can further change the appearance of the printout by using the **File, Page Setup** command, or clicking at the **Page Setup** button of the Print dialogue box. Either of these causes the following dialogue box to appear on the screen.

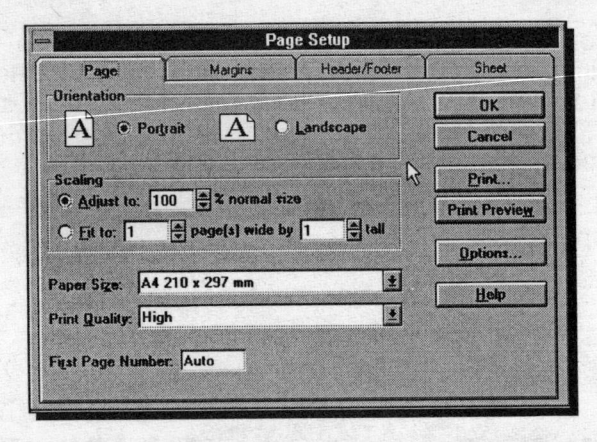

By selecting the appropriate Tab on this dialogue box, you can change your **Page** settings, page **Margins**, specify a **Header/Footer**, and control how a **Sheet** should be printed. Each Tab displays a different dialogue box, appropriate to the function at hand. In the **Header/Footer** dialogue box you can even click the down-arrow against the Header and Footer boxes to display a suggested list for these, appropriate to the work you are doing, the person responsible for it and even the date it is being carried out! Try it.

A very useful feature of Excel is the **Scaling** facility shown in the above dialogue box. You can print actual size or a percentage of it, or you can choose to fit your worksheet on to one page which allows Excel to scale your work automatically.

To preview a worksheet, click the 'Print Preview' icon on the Toolbar, shown here, or use the **Print Preview** button on the Print or Page Setup dialogue box, or use the **File, Print Preview** command.

8. ADVANCED SPREADSHEETS

Enhancing a Worksheet

You can make your work look more professional by adopting various enhancements, such as single and double line cell borders, shading certain cells, and adding meaningful headers and footers.

However, with Excel you can select easily a pre-defined style to display your work on both the screen and on paper. To do this, place the active cell within the table (or range) you want to format, say C5, then select the **Format, AutoFormat** which will cause the following dialogue box to appear on the screen, displaying a sample of the chosen table format. In this way you can choose what best suits your needs.

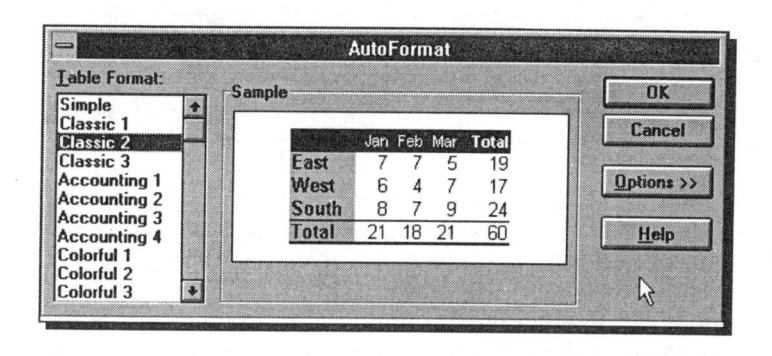

Next, reduce the title of the worksheet to PROJECT ANALYSIS, then centre it within the range A1:E1, by first selecting the range, then clicking the 'Centre Across Columns' icon, shown here, which causes the title to centre within the specified range.

Finally, save the worksheet as **project4**, before going on.

Header and Footer Icons and Codes:

With the help of header and footer icons and their codes, shown below, you can position text or automatically insert information at the top or bottom of a report printout.

To add a header to our printed example, use the **File, Page Set**u**p** command and click on the **Header/Footer** Tab, press the **Custom Header** button and type the information displayed below in the Left Section and Right Section of the Header box:

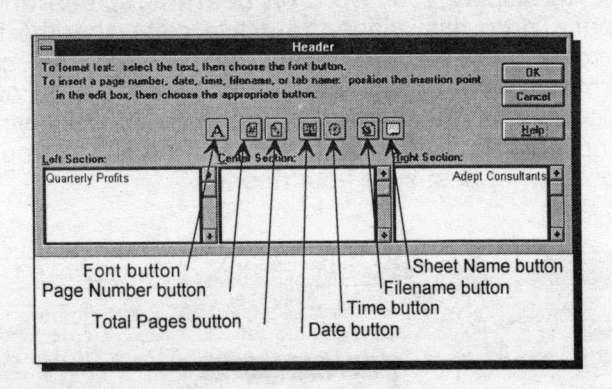

While the insertion pointer is in, say, the Centre Section of the Header box, pointing and clicking on the 'Sheet Name' button, inserts the &[Tab] code which has the effect of inserting the sheet name of the current active sheet at the time of printing. The first icon button displays the Font dialogue box, while the others display the codes listed below.

Code	*Action*
&[Page]	Inserts a page number.
&[Pages]	Inserts the total number of pages.
&[Date]	Inserts the current date.
&[Time]	Inserts the current time.
&[File]	Inserts the filename of the current workbook.

Setting a Print Area:

To select a smaller print area than the current worksheet, select the required area by highlighting the starting cell of the area and dragging the mouse, or using the **<Shift+Arrows>**, to highlight the block, and use the **File, Print** command which displays the following dialogue box:

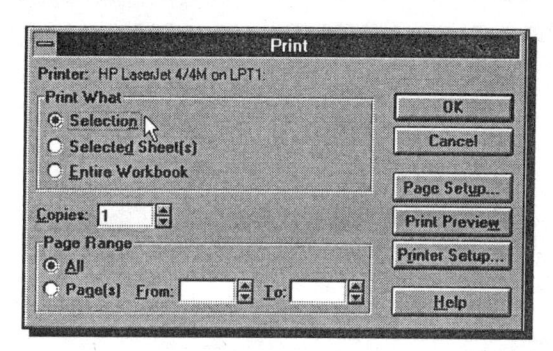

Choose the **Selection** button in the **Print What** box, and either press the **Print Preview** or the **OK** button to preview your report on screen or print it on paper.

Once in preview mode, the following icons are available to you.

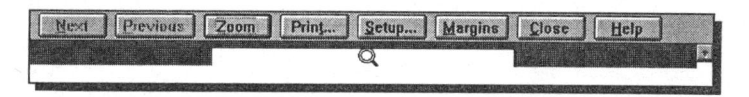

The first two allow you to change sheets, while the next one allows you to review your print output magnified or at full page size - when in full page size, the mouse pointer looks like a magnifying glass, as above. The next three icons can be used to print, change page settings, or to display the margins. To leave the preview option, press the Close icon.

If you want to return to the option of printing selected sheets or the entire workbook, then click the appropriate button in the **Print What** box of the Print dialogue box.

The default selection in the **Print What** box is **Selected Sheet(s)** which is also what will be printed out if you click the 'Print' icon, shown here.

If you have included headers and footers, these will be printed out irrespective of whether you choose to print a selected range or a selected worksheet.

Printing our worksheet produces the following page:

Quarterly Profits				Adept Consultants
	Jan	Feb	Mar	1st Quarter
Income	£14,000.00	£15,000.00	£16,000.00	£45,000.00
Costs:				
Wages	£ 2,000.00	£ 3,000.00	£ 4,000.00	£ 9,000.00
Travel	£ 400.00	£ 500.00	£ 600.00	£ 1,500.00
Rent	£ 300.00	£ 300.00	£ 300.00	£ 900.00
Heat/Light	£ 150.00	£ 200.00	£ 130.00	£ 480.00
Phone/Fax	£ 250.00	£ 300.00	£ 350.00	£ 900.00
Adverts	£ 1,100.00	£ 1,200.00	£ 1,300.00	£ 3,600.00
Total Costs	£ 4,200.00	£ 5,500.00	£ 6,680.00	£16,380.00
Profit	£ 9,800.00	£ 9,500.00	£ 9,320.00	£28,620.00
Cumulative	£ 9,800.00	£19,300.00	£28,620.00	

15/9/95	Page 1

3-Dimensional Worksheets

In Excel, a 3-dimensional file is one made up with a series of flat 2-dimensional sheets stacked 'on top of each other'. Each sheet is the same size, and in itself, behaves the same as the more ordinary worksheets. As mentioned previously, each separate sheet in a file has its own Tab identifier at the bottom of the screen. Ranges can be set to span several different sheets to build up 3-dimensional blocks of data. These blocks can then be manipulated, copied, or moved to other locations in the file. A cell can reference any other cell in the file, no matter what sheet it is on, and an extended range of functions can be used to process these 3-dimensional ranges.

Manipulating Ranges:

The best way to demonstrate a new idea is to work through an example. We will use the worksheet saved under **project4** (see end of previous chapter). Next, start Excel, use the **File, Open** command, or click the 'file open' icon, and select **project4**. On pressing <Enter>, the worksheet is displayed on the screen as shown below.

	A	B	C	D	E	F	G	H
1	PROJECT ANALYSIS 1st Quarter							
2								
3		Jan	Feb	Mar	1st Quarter			
4	Income	£14,000.00	£15,000.00	£16,000.00	£45,000.00			
5	Costs:							
6	Wages	£ 2,000.00	£ 3,000.00	£ 4,000.00	£ 9,000.00			
7	Travel	£ 400.00	£ 500.00	£ 600.00	£ 1,500.00			
8	Rent	£ 300.00	£ 300.00	£ 300.00	£ 900.00			
9	Heat/Light	£ 150.00	£ 200.00	£ 130.00	£ 480.00			
10	Phone/Fax	£ 250.00	£ 300.00	£ 350.00	£ 900.00			
11	Adverts	£ 1,100.00	£ 1,200.00	£ 1,300.00	£ 3,600.00			
12	Total Costs	£ 4,200.00	£ 5,500.00	£ 6,680.00	£16,380.00			
13	Profit	£ 9,800.00	£ 9,500.00	£ 9,320.00	£28,620.00			
14	Cumulative	£ 9,800.00	£19,300.00	£28,620.00				
15								

Copying Sheets into a Workbook

We will now fill another three sheets behind the present one, in order to include information about ADEPT Consultants' trading during the other three quarters of the year. The easiest way of doing this is by copying the information in Sheet1, including the formatting and the entered formulae, onto the other three sheets, then edit the numerical information in these appropriately.

To simplify this operation, Excel has a facility which allows you to copy a sheet into a workbook. There are two ways of doing this: (a) with the mouse, or (b) using the menus.

With the mouse, make the sheet you want to copy the current sheet, then press the <Ctrl> key, and while keeping it pressed, point with the mouse on the Tab of Sheet1 and drag it to the right, as follows:

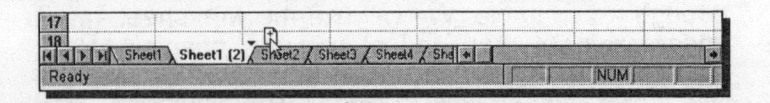

A small black triangle indicates the place where the copy will be inserted. If you insert a copy, say before Sheet2, when you release the mouse button the inserted sheet will be given the name Sheet1(2), as shown above, where we are about to insert a second copy before Sheet2 which will be named Sheet1(3).

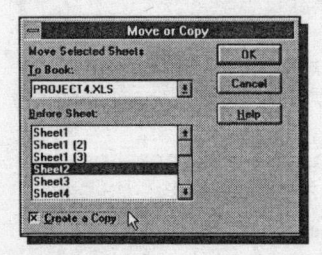

To copy a sheet with the use of menus, select the **Edit, Move or Copy Sheet** command, then highlight Sheet2 in the **Before Sheet** list of the displayed dialogue box, then check the **Create a Copy** option at the bottom of the dialogue box, and press the **OK** button. Sheet1(4) will be inserted in the Workbook.

Next, double click the Tabs of these four new sheets and change their names to 'Quarter 1', 'Quarter 2', 'Quarter 3' and 'Quarter 4', respectively.

The contents of the second sheet should be as follows:

	A	B	C	D	E	F
1	PROJECT ANALYSIS 2nd Quarter					
2						
3		Apr	May	Jun	2nd Quarter	
4	Income	£15,500.00	£16,000.00	£16,500.00	£48,000.00	
5	Costs:					
6	Wages	£ 3,500.00	£ 4,000.00	£ 4,500.00	£12,000.00	
7	Travel	£ 500.00	£ 550.00	£ 580.00	£ 1,630.00	
8	Rent	£ 300.00	£ 300.00	£ 300.00	£ 900.00	
9	Heat/Light	£ 150.00	£ 120.00	£ 100.00	£ 370.00	
10	Phone/Fax	£ 300.00	£ 350.00	£ 400.00	£ 1,050.00	
11	Adverts	£ 1,250.00	£ 1,300.00	£ 1,350.00	£ 3,900.00	
12	Total Costs	£ 6,000.00	£ 6,620.00	£ 7,230.00	£19,850.00	
13	Profit	£ 9,500.00	£ 9,380.00	£ 9,270.00	£28,150.00	
14	Cumulative	£ 9,500.00	£18,880.00	£28,150.00		

The easiest way to enter these 2nd Quarter results is to edit the copied data (from Quarter 1) by either using the EDIT key (**F2**), or double-clicking the cell you want to edit. You should now be in a position to complete editing the sheets of the other quarters. Be extra careful, from now on, to check the identification Tab at the bottom of the screen, so as not to get the sheets mixed up. You do not want to spend time editing the wrong worksheet!

After building up the four worksheets (one for each quarter - see beginning of next chapter for details on the 3rd and 4th quarters) save the file as **project5**.

Linking Sheets

A consolidation sheet could be placed in front of our 'stack' of data sheets to show a full year's results, by making a copy of the 1st Quarter sheet and placing it in front of it. Next, delete the entries in columns B to E, and name it 'Consolidation'.

We are now in a position to link the consolidation sheet to the other quarterly data sheets so that the information contained on them is automatically summarised and updated on it. The quarter totals in columns E of sheets Quarter 1, Quarter 2, Quarter 3, and Quarter 4, can be copied in turn to the clipboard using the **Edit, Copy** command, and then pasted to the appropriate column of the Consolidate sheet with the use of the **Edit, Paste Special** command and pressing the **Paste Link** button on the displayed dialogue box.

Note: Empty cells linked with this method, like those in cells E5 of each quarter, appear as 0 (zero) in the Consolidation sheet, and cannot be removed. To correct this, copy each column E of each quarter in two stages; E3:E4, then E6:E13.

Next, insert appropriate formulae in row 14 to correctly calculate the cumulative values in the consolidation sheet. The result should be as follows:

	E13		{='Quarter 4'!$E$6:$E$13}						
	A	B	C	D	E	F	G	H	I
1		PROJECT ANALYSIS - Year Summary							
2									
3		1st Quarter	2nd Quarter	3rd Quarter	4th Quarter				
4	Income	£ 45,000.00	£ 48,000.00	£ 52,500.00	£ 57,000.00				
5	Costs:								
6	Wages	£ 9,000.00	£ 12,000.00	£ 13,500.00	£ 15,000.00				
7	Travel	£ 1,500.00	£ 1,630.00	£ 1,930.00	£ 2,000.00				
8	Rent	£ 900.00	£ 900.00	£ 900.00	£ 900.00				
9	Heat/Light	£ 480.00	£ 370.00	£ 250.00	£ 610.00				
10	Phone/Fax	£ 900.00	£ 1,050.00	£ 1,150.00	£ 1,270.00				
11	Adverts	£ 3,600.00	£ 3,900.00	£ 4,350.00	£ 4,510.00				
12	Total Costs	£ 16,380.00	£ 19,850.00	£ 22,080.00	£ 24,290.00				
13	Profit	£ 28,620.00	£ 28,150.00	£ 30,420.00	£ 32,710.00				
14	Cumulative	£ 28,620.00	£ 56,770.00	£ 87,190.00	£119,900.00				
15									

Finally, save the resultant workbook as **project6**.

Relative and Absolute Cell Addresses

Entering a mathematical expression into Excel, such as the formula in cell C14 which was

=B14+C13

causes Excel to interpret it as 'add the contents of cell one column to the left of the current position, to the contents of cell one row above the current position'. In this way, when the formula was later copied into cell address D14, the contents of the cell relative to the left position of D14 (i.e. C14) and the contents of the cell one row above it (i.e. D13) were used, instead of the original cell addresses entered in C14. This is relative addressing.

To see the effect of relative versus absolute addressing, copy the formula in cell C14 into C17, as shown below:

	A	B	C	D	E	F
1	PROJECT ANALYSIS - Year Summary					
2						
3		1st Quarter	2nd Quarter	3rd Quarter	4th Quarter	
4	Income	£ 45,000.00	£ 48,000.00	£ 52,500.00	£ 57,000.00	
5	Costs:					
6	Wages	£ 9,000.00	£ 12,000.00	£ 13,500.00	£ 15,000.00	
7	Travel	£ 1,500.00	£ 1,630.00	£ 1,930.00	£ 2,000.00	
8	Rent	£ 900.00	£ 900.00	£ 900.00	£ 900.00	
9	Heat/Light	£ 480.00	£ 370.00	£ 250.00	£ 610.00	
10	Phone/Fax	£ 900.00	£ 1,050.00	£ 1,150.00	£ 1,270.00	
11	Adverts	£ 3,600.00	£ 3,900.00	£ 4,350.00	£ 4,510.00	
12	Total Costs	£ 16,380.00	£ 19,850.00	£ 22,080.00	£ 24,290.00	
13	Profit	£ 28,620.00	£ 28,150.00	£ 30,420.00	£ 32,710.00	
14	Cumulative	£ 28,620.00	£ 56,770.00	£ 87,190.00	£119,900.00	
15						
16						
17			£ -			

Cell reference: C17, Formula: =B17+C16

Note that in cell C14 the formula was =B14+C13. However, when copied into cell C17 the formula appears as

=B17+C16

because it has been interpreted as relative addressing. In this case, no value appears in cell C17 because we are attempting to add two blank cells.

Now change the formula in C14 by editing it to

=$B$14+$C$13

which is interpreted as absolute addressing. Copying this formula into cell C17 calculates the correct result. Highlight cell C17 and observe the cell references in its formula; they have not changed from those of cell C14.

The $ sign must prefix both the column reference and the row reference. Mixed cell addressing is permitted; as for example when a column address reference is needed to be taken as absolute, while a row address reference is needed to be taken as relative. In such a case, the column letter is prefixed by the $ sign.

Freezing Panes on Screen

Sometimes there might be too much information on screen and attempting to see a certain part of a sheet might cause the labels associated with that information to scroll off the screen.

To freeze column (or row) labels on a worksheet, move the cell pointer to the right (or below) the column (or row) which you want to freeze the labels on the screen, and use the

Window, Freeze Panes

command. Everything to the left of (or above) the cell pointer will freeze on the screen.

9. SPREADSHEET CHARTS

Excel allows information within a worksheet to be represented in graphical form which makes data more accessible to non-expert users who might not be familiar with the spreadsheet format. The saying 'a picture is worth a thousand words', applies equally well to charts and figures.

The package allows the use of several chart and graph types, including area, bar, column, line, doughnut, radar, XY, pie, combination, and several 3-D options of these charts. In all, Excel allows fifteen different types of charts, with a total of 102 pre-defined formats, which can be selected with the use of an appropriate icon, made available to you once you have selected the data you want to chart and indicated the place you want the chart to appear on your worksheet.

These charts (you can have several per worksheet) can be displayed on screen at the same time as the worksheet from which they were derived since they appear in their own 'chart' frame and can be embedded anywhere on a worksheet. Furthermore, they can be sent to an appropriate output device, such as a plotter or printer. Although this charting module rivals a stand alone graphics package, and one could write a separate book on it, an attempt will be made to present its basics, in the space available.

Preparing for a Column Chart

In order to illustrate some of the graphing capabilities of Excel, we will now plot the income of the consulting company we discussed in the **project6** file. However, before we can go on, you will need to complete the entries for the last two quarters of trading of the Adept Consultants' example, if you haven't already done so, as follows:

	Jul	Aug	Sep	Oct	Nov	Dec
Income	17,000	17,500	18,000	18,500	19,000	19,500
Costs:						
Wages	4,000	4,500	5,000	4,500	5,000	5,500
Travel	600	650	680	630	670	700
Rent	300	300	300	300	300	300
Heat/Light	50	80	120	160	200	250
Phone/Fax	350	380	420	400	420	450
Adverts	1,400	1,450	1,500	1,480	1,500	1,530

Next, link the quarterly totals to the consolidation sheet and calculate the year's total, and save as **project7**.

F6		=SUM(B6:E6)			
			PROJECT7.XLS		
	A	B	C	D	E	F
---	---	---	---	---	---	---
1		*PROJECT ANALYSIS - Year Summary*				
2						
3		1st Quarter	2nd Quarter	3rd Quarter	4th Quarter	
4	Income	£ 45,000.00	£ 48,000.00	£ 52,500.00	£ 57,000.00	£202,500.00
5	Costs:					
6	Wages	£ 9,000.00	£ 12,000.00	£ 13,500.00	£ 15,000.00	£ 49,500.00
7	Travel	£ 1,500.00	£ 1,630.00	£ 1,930.00	£ 2,000.00	£ 7,060.00
8	Rent	£ 900.00	£ 900.00	£ 900.00	£ 900.00	£ 3,600.00
9	Heat/Light	£ 480.00	£ 370.00	£ 250.00	£ 610.00	£ 1,710.00
10	Phone/Fax	£ 900.00	£ 1,050.00	£ 1,150.00	£ 1,270.00	£ 4,370.00
11	Adverts	£ 3,600.00	£ 3,900.00	£ 4,350.00	£ 4,510.00	£ 16,360.00
12	Total Costs	£ 16,380.00	£ 19,850.00	£ 22,080.00	£ 24,290.00	£ 82,600.00
13	Profit	£ 28,620.00	£ 28,150.00	£ 30,420.00	£ 32,710.00	£119,900.00
14	Cumulative	£ 28,620.00	£ 56,770.00	£ 87,190.00	£119,900.00	
15						
16						

Consolidation / Quarter 1 / Quarter 2 / Quarter 3 / Quarter 4

Now we need to select the range of the data we want to graph. The range of data to be graphed in Excel does not have to be contiguous for each graph, as with some other spreadsheets. With Excel, you select your data from different parts of a sheet with the <Ctrl> key pressed down. This method has the advantage of automatic recalculation should any changes be made to the original data. You could also collect data from different sheets to one 'graphing' sheet by linking them as we did with the consolidation sheet.

If you don't want the chart to be recalculated when you do this, then you must use the **Edit, Copy** and **Edit, Paste Special** commands and choose the **Values** option from the displayed dialogue box, which copies a selected range to a specified target area of the worksheet and converts formulae to values. This is necessary, as cells containing formulae cannot be pasted directly since it would cause the relative cell addresses to adjust to the new locations and each formula would then recalculate a new value for each cell and give wrong results.

The ChartWizard

To obtain a chart of 'Income' versus 'Quarters', select the data in cell range A3..E4, then either click at the ChartWizard, shown here, or use the **Insert, Chart, On This Sheet** command. On doing so, the cursor changes (once in the worksheet area) to a small column chart, as shown below.

	A	B	C	D	E	F	G
1	PROJECT ANALYSIS - Year Summary						
2							
3		1st Quarter	2nd Quarter	3rd Quarter	4th Quarter		
4	Income	£ 45,000.00	£ 48,000.00	£ 52,500.00	£ 57,000.00	£202,500.00	
5	Costs:						
6	Wages	£ 9,000.00	£ 12,000.00	£ 13,500.00	£ 15,000.00	£ 49,500.00	
7	Travel	£ 1,500.00	£ 1,630.00	£ 1,930.00	£ 2,000.00	£ 7,060.00	
8	Rent	£ 900.00	£ 900.00	£ 900.00	£ 900.00	£ 3,600.00	
9	Heat/Light	£ 480.00	£ 370.00	£ 250.00	£ 610.00	£ 1,710.00	
10	Phone/Fax	£ 900.00	£ 1,050.00	£ 1,150.00	£ 1,270.00	£ 4,370.00	
11	Adverts	£ 3,600.00	£ 3,900.00	£ 4,350.00	£ 4,510.00	£ 16,360.00	
12	Total Costs	£ 16,380.00	£ 19,850.00	£ 22,080.00	£ 24,290.00	£ 82,600.00	
13	Profit	£ 28,620.00	£ 28,150.00	£ 30,420.00	£ 32,710.00	£119,900.00	
14	Cumulative	£ 28,620.00	£ 56,770.00	£ 87,190.00	£119,900.00		
15							

Now move the mouse pointer to the place you want to position the top-left corner of your chart, press the left mouse button and while keeping it pressed, drag the mouse down and to the right to form a dotted rectangle within which the chart will appear automatically once you release the mouse button and have selected the chart type. The result could be as follows:

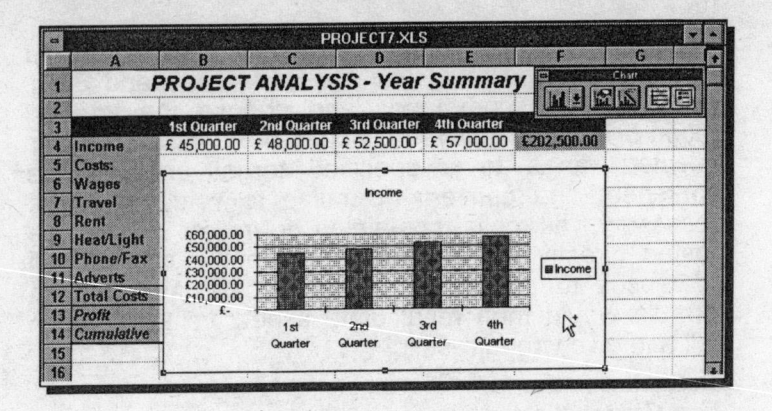

Note that while the frame containing a chart is selected (you can tell from the presence of the small black squares around it), a special Chart toolbar, shown here, appears above and to the right of it. These icons have the following function:

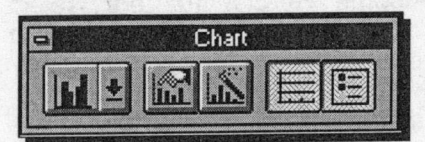

Produces a drop-down series of icons from which you can select the chart type.

Allows you to select the default chart.

Allows you to select ChartWizard's dialogue boxes to specify the data range for the chart and whether the data series is in rows or columns.

Toggles the horizontal gridlines on or off.

Toggles the legends on or off.

You can change the size of a selected chart by dragging the small four-headed arrow pointer (which appears when the mouse pointer is placed at the edges of the frame and on the small black boxes). You can also move the whole frame to a new position by clicking within it and dragging it to its new position.

As an example of what you can do with a chart, let us select a pattern to be used as a frame, by using the **Format, Object** command and in the displayed Format Object dialogue box, shown below, select **Custom** under the Patterns tab and choose the 7th **Style**, the 4th **Weight** line, and click at the **Shadow** box to cross it. Next, change the chart type to a 3D column chart, to obtain the displayed chart overleaf.

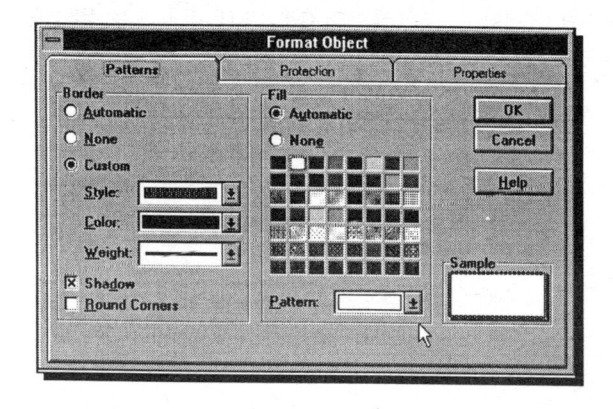

Try it, then change the first quarter income from £45,000 to £55,000 (on the Quarter 1 sheet), and watch how the change is reflected on the redrawn graph on the Consolidation sheet displayed on the next page.

Finally, revert to the original entry for the first quarter's income, change your chart back to a simple column type, and then save your work again under the filename **project7** by simply pressing the Save icon shown here. Your current work will be saved to disc replacing the previous version under the same filename.

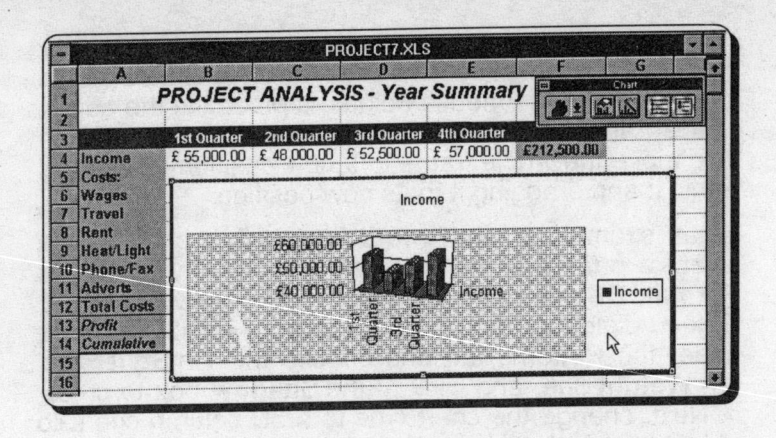

When Excel creates a chart, it plots each row or column of data in the selected range as a 'data series', such as a group of bars, lines, etc. A chart can contain many data series, but Excel charts data according to the following rules:

1. If the selected range contains more rows than columns of data, Excel plots the data series by columns.

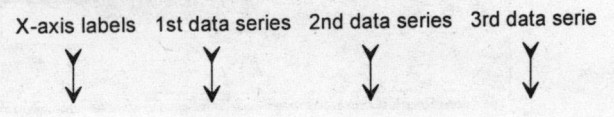

   X-axis labels   1st data series   2nd data series   3rd data serie
   ↓   ↓   ↓   ↓

2. If the selected range contains more columns than rows of data, or the same number of columns and rows, Excel plots the data series by rows.

   Legend   X-axis labels   →
   labels   1st data series   →
             2nd data series   →

If you select a range to chart which includes column and row headings, and text above or to the left of the numeric data, Excel uses the text to create the axis labels, legends, and title.

If your data selection does not obey these rules, you must use the ChartWizard, and tell Excel how your data series is structured in the 4th displayed dialogue box. The ChartWizard opens 5 dialogue boxes altogether, as follows:

1. Range selection

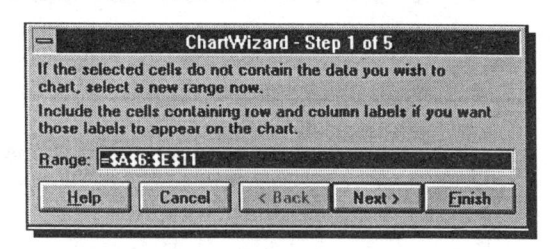

2. Chart type selection

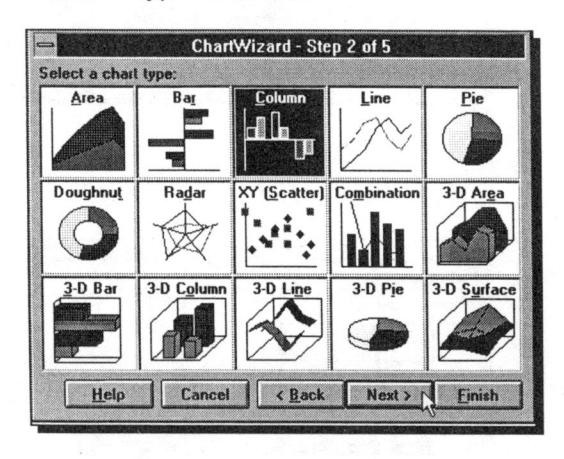

3. Format selection for chosen chart

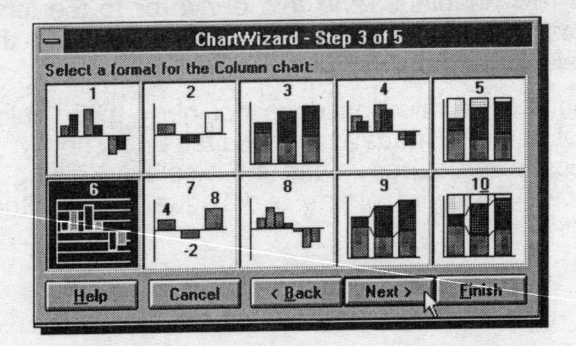

4. Data series specification

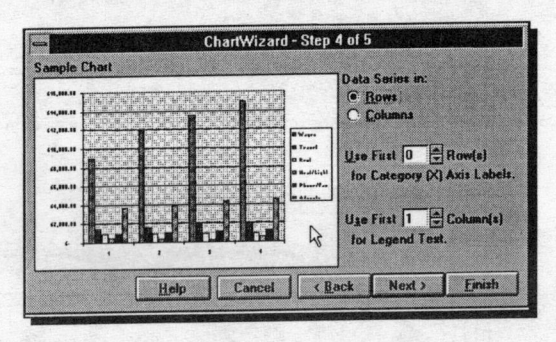

5. Legend and title selection

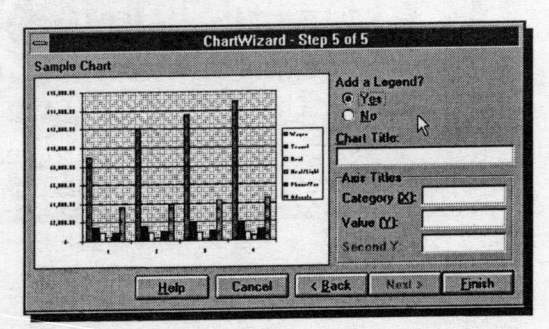

Saving and Naming Charts:

When you save a worksheet, the chart or charts you have created are saved with it. Charts are numbered automatically as you create them and are given the default name Chart#, where # is a sequential number starting with 1. If you have created a chart and subsequently deleted it, the next chart created will be named one number above the deleted chart.

If you prefer, you can rename charts so that they have names more relevant to what they represent. To do so, select the chart by clicking within its boundaries, then click the Reference Indicator (which should display the name Chart#), and type a new name.

As we will be creating quite a number of charts, rename the existing Chart1 to Income_bar.

Pre-defined Chart Types

To select a different type of chart, click the ChartWizard icon shown here, or select the **Insert, Chart** command. The 2nd ChartWizard dialogue box displayed previously, lists 15 different chart options, but 6 of these are 3D versions of Area, Bar, Column, Line, Pie, and Surface charts. The nine main graph-types are normally used to describe the following relationships between data:

Area: for showing a volume relationship between two series, such as production or sales, over a given length of time.

Bar: for comparing differences in data - non-continuous data that are not related over time - by depicting changes in horizontal bars to show positive and negative variations from a given position.

Column: for comparing separate items - non-continuous data which are related over time - by depicting changes in vertical bars to show positive and negative variations from a given position.

Line: for showing continuous changes in data with time.

Pie: for comparing parts with the whole. You can use this type of chart when you want to compare the percentage of an item from a single series of data with the whole series.

Doughnut: for comparing parts with the whole. Similar to pie charts, but can depict more than one series of data.

Radar: for plotting one series of data as angle values defined in radians, against one or more series defined in terms of a radius.

XY: for showing scatter relationships between X and Y. Scatter charts are used to depict items which are not related over time.

Combination: for comparing different chart types or different scaling systems by overlaying different type of charts (up to a maximum of four).

You can change the type of chart by selecting one of the fifteen alternate chart types (including the 3D variations of Area, Bar, Column, Line, Pie, and Surface) from the 2nd ChartWizard dialogue box, pressing the **Next** button and choosing one of the pre-defined charts from the displayed selection, provided your data fits the selection.

Customising a Chart

In order to customise a chart, you need to know how to add legends, titles, text labels, arrows, and how to change the colour and pattern of the chart background, plot areas and chart markers, and how to select, move and size chart objects.

Drawing a Multiple Column Chart:

As an exercise, we will consider a new column chart which deals with the quarterly 'Costs' of Adept Consultants. To achieve this, first select the cell range A3:E3 then, while holding the <Ctrl> key down, select the costs range A6:E11 and press the ChartWizard icon (or use the **Insert, Chart** command), and select the target area. The column chart of the 6 different quarterly costs will be drawn automatically, as displayed in the 4th ChartWizard dialogue box shown in the composite screen dump below. Note that the highlighting of the selected range actually disappears once the target area is defined.

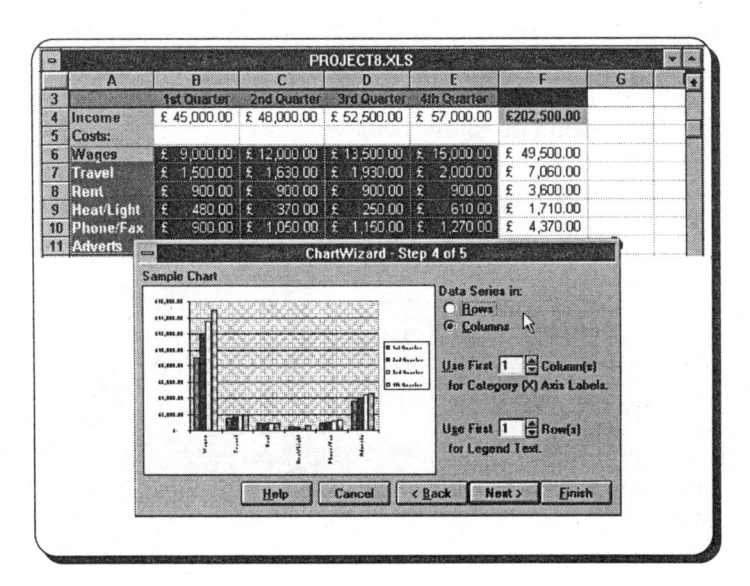

Because the selected range contains more rows than columns of data, Excel follows the 1st rule of data series selection which, however, might not be what you want.

To have the 'quarters' appearing on the x-axis and the 'costs' as the legends, we need to tell Excel that our data series is in rows by clicking the **Row** button on the 4th ChartWizard dialogue box. Immediately this is done the column chart changes to:

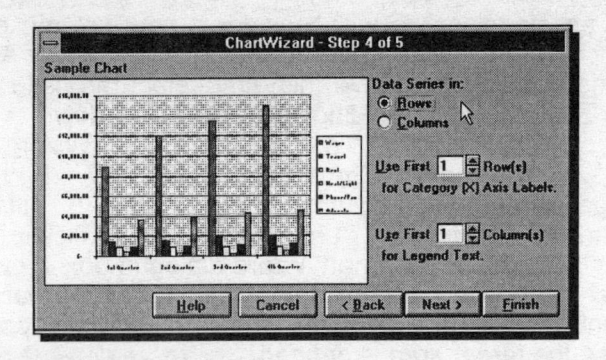

Now click the **Next** button, and type in the **Chart Title** box of the 5th ChartWizard dialogue box the heading 'PROJECT ANALYSIS - Year Summary', followed by the **Axis Titles** as shown below.

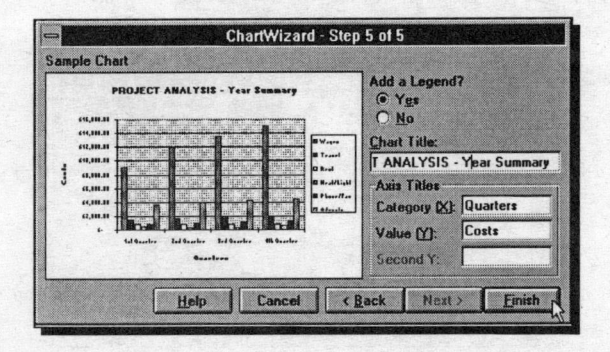

When you click the **Finish** button, the following chart appears on the screen:

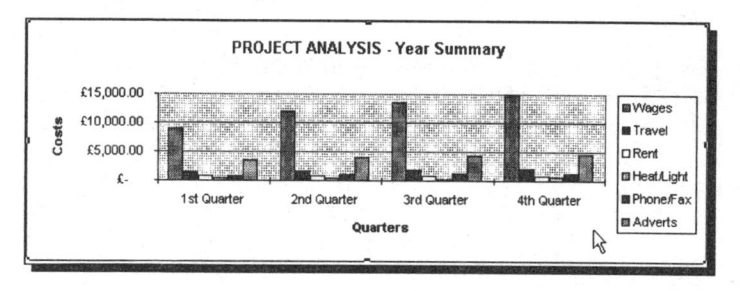

If you make a mistake and you want to try again, make sure the unwanted chart is selected, then press the <Del> key. Once you are satisfied with your efforts, name your chart Costs_bar and save your work under the filename **project8**.

Changing a Title and an Axis Label:

To change a title or an axis label within a chart, double-click inside the chart. Once this is done, clicking at the title, the X- or Y-axis label, or the legends, reveals that these are individual objects (they are surrounded by small black squares) and you can re-position them, or change their font and point size, as shown below.

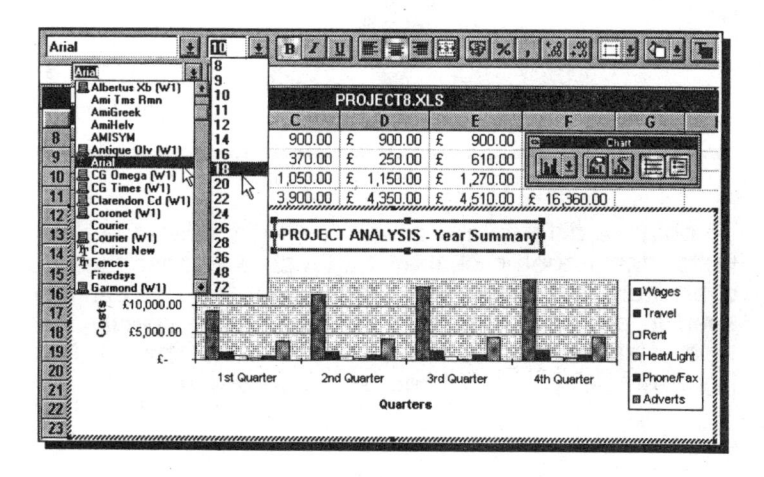

Once you have selected a chart, by double-clicking inside it, the **Insert** command reveals a changed drop-down sub-menu from the usual one, as shown here. From this sub-menu you can enter titles or axis labels, enter data labels, add chart legends, specify which axis to display, specify which gridlines to display, or insert a picture from a file. You can even select new data to add to your chart.

Drawing a Pie Chart:

To change the chart type, simply select the chart, then click the Chart Type icon on the **Chart** Toolbar and choose the pie picture from the displayed drop-down list. If the selected chart was the 'quarterly costs' chart, then on pressing the **OK** button the chart would be redrawn to the following:

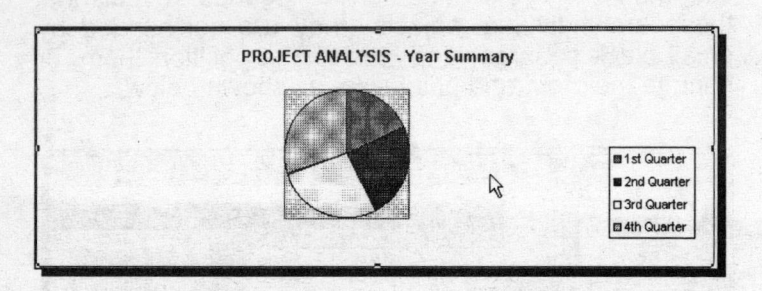

PROJECT ANALYSIS - Year Summary

- 1st Quarter
- 2nd Quarter
- 3rd Quarter
- 4th Quarter

To obtain a different pie chart, you must select the data range again, then click the ChartWizard, choose the pie chart from the displayed chart types, then select the specific pie chart that best fits your data, specify the type of series data as 'rows', and give the chart a title. For example, you could choose the following:

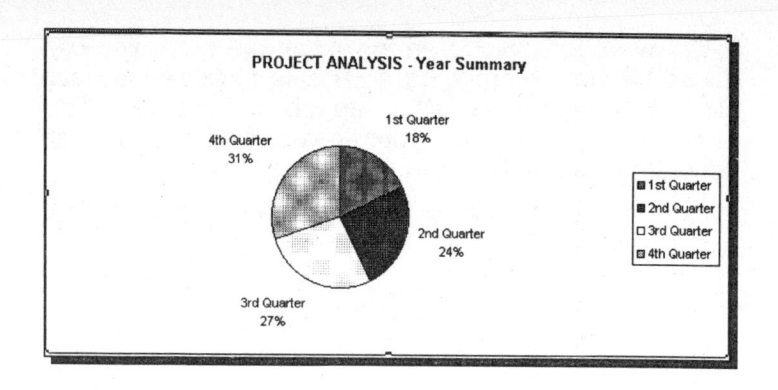

PROJECT ANALYSIS - Year Summary

- 1st Quarter: 18%
- 2nd Quarter: 24%
- 3rd Quarter: 27%
- 4th Quarter: 31%

This chart tells us that the costs have been increasing from 18% for the 1st quarter to 31% for the 4th quarter, in a clockwise manner, but it doesn't tell us much more.

As a last example in chart drawing, we will use the same data range of the costs from the worksheet to plot a 3-D pie chart.

The steps are the same as before, but for the 3-D option and specifying the type of series data as 'columns'. The result should be as follows:

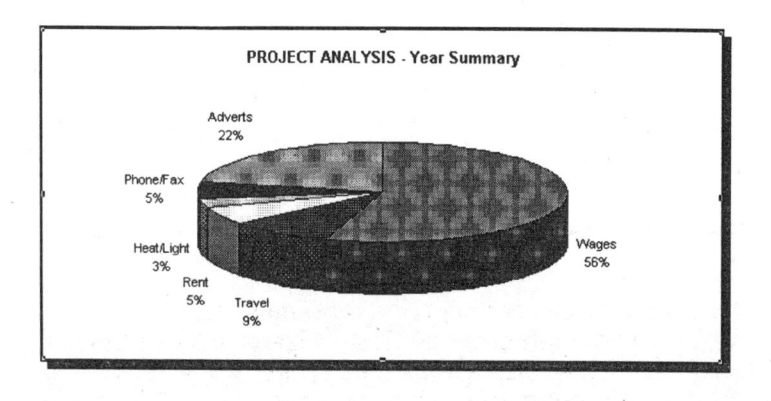

PROJECT ANALYSIS - Year Summary

- Adverts: 22%
- Phone/Fax: 5%
- Heat/Light: 3%
- Rent: 5%
- Travel: 9%
- Wages: 56%

It is now obvious that the information contained in this chart is much more than in the 2-D version.

If you want to explode an individual pie slice, you can do so by simply dragging it. This is possible as each slice is treated as a separate object, but you must increase the size of your chart before you can accurately pinpoint the required slice.

Finally, name the pie chart Costs_pie and save your worksheet as **project9**.

* * *

Excel has many more features than the ones we have introduced in this book. For example, you could use Excel's database and macro capabilities, and also explore its various tools, such as the Auditor, the Goal Seek, the What-if Tables, and the Solver. We hope we have given you sufficient basic knowledge to be able to explore these topics by yourself.

However, if you would prefer to be guided through these topics, then may we suggest you look up the later chapters of the book *Excel 5 Explained* (BP352), also published by BERNARD BABANI (publishing) Ltd.

10. THE POWERPOINT ENVIRONMENT

Microsoft PowerPoint is a powerful and versatile Graphics Presentation package which, however, is the least used of the MS-Office components.

The key element of PowerPoint is the Slide Show and the production of ancillary material, such as scripted notes to accompany each slide, laser copies of slides, and an outline view of all the information in the presentation. However, Microsoft uses the word slide to refer to each individual page of presentation and you can format the output for overhead projector acetates, or electronic presentation on screen.

In addition, you can apply the skills you have already gained in using Word and Excel and use material created in these applications within PowerPoint.

Starting the PowerPoint Program

To start PowerPoint, start Windows, open the Windows Program Manager, and if you are using a mouse, point to the Microsoft PowerPoint icon, shown here, and double-click the left mouse button.

Although you could start PowerPoint using the usual keyboard procedure, there is not much point doing so, unless you simply wanted to learn about the program, as a mouse is mandatory, if you are going to do anything at all with it.

When PowerPoint is loaded, a screen displays with similar Title bar, Menu bar, Toolbar and Formatting bar to those of Word and Excel. Obviously there are differences, but that is to be expected as PowerPoint serves a different purpose to the other programs.

The PowerPoint Screen

The opening screen of PowerPoint is shown below. The program follows the usual Microsoft Windows conventions with which you should be very familiar by now. Scroll bars and scroll buttons appear within the window in which you load a presentation.

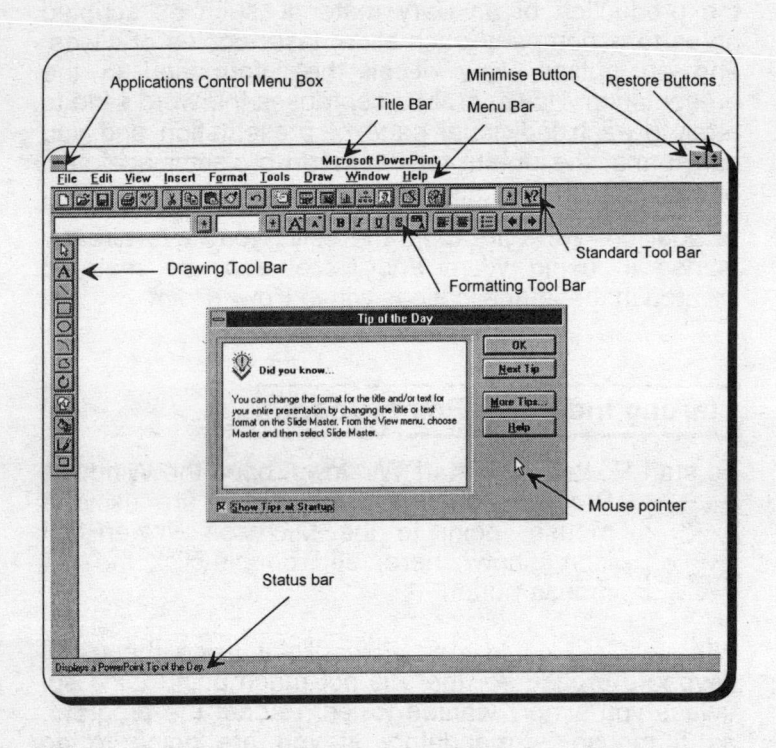

After clicking the **OK** button on the Tip of the Day box, the program displays the PowerPoint dialogue box, shown on the next page. The same dialogue box also displays when you click the New icon, shown here, but its name changes to New Presentation. The options on this dialogue box make it easy for you to start your presentation.

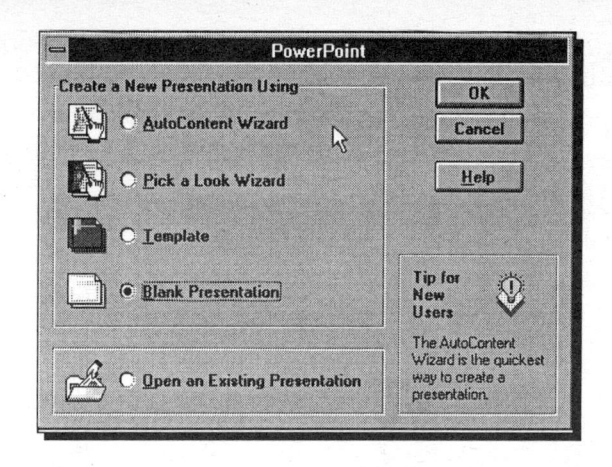

These options allow you to create a new presentation, as follows:

AutoContent Wizard	Activates a Wizard that helps you determine the content and organisation of your presentation.
Pick a Look Wizard	Activates a Wizard that helps you determine the look and feel of your presentation.
Template	Allows you to select a presentation template that determines the colour scheme, fonts, and other design features of the presentation.
Blank Presentation	Allows you to start with a blank presentation with all values for colour scheme, fonts, and other design features set to default values.

The last option allows you to either Open an Existing Presentation or use the Current Presentation Format.

The only new item on the screen is the Draw Toolbar on the left of the display. It has the following functions:

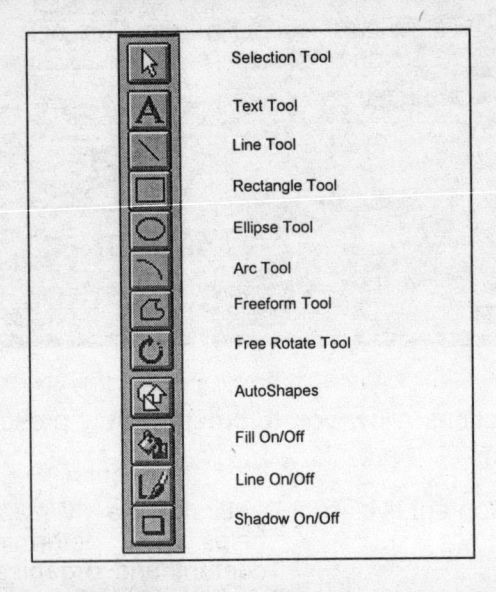

- Selection Tool
- Text Tool
- Line Tool
- Rectangle Tool
- Ellipse Tool
- Arc Tool
- Freeform Tool
- Free Rotate Tool
- AutoShapes
- Fill On/Off
- Line On/Off
- Shadow On/Off

To use these various tools, you must have a Presentation window open. The one below can be found in the **samples** subdirectory of the **powerpnt** directory. Also note the additional Slide View buttons.

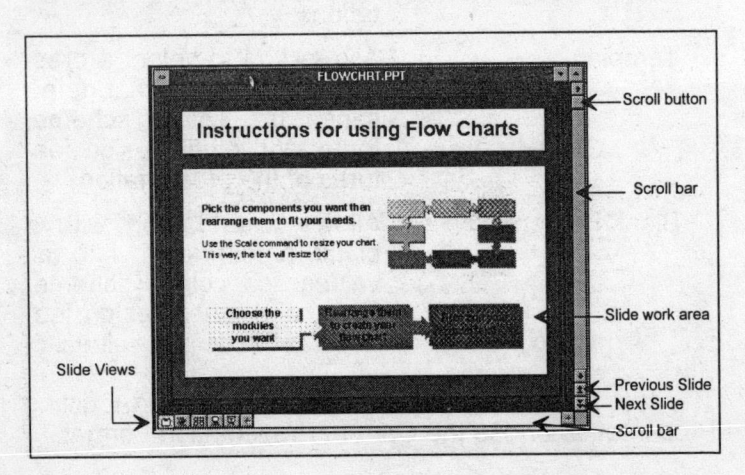

PowerPoint Views

The Slide View bar at the bottom left corner of the Presentation window, is shown enlarged below.

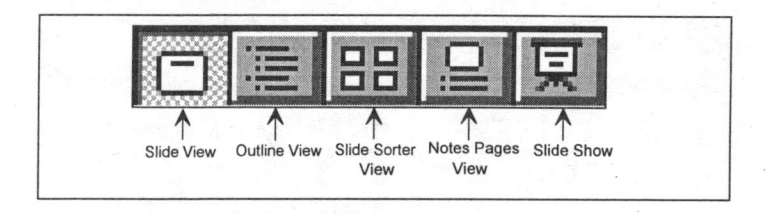

Slide View   Outline View   Slide Sorter View   Notes Pages View   Slide Show

These five Slide View buttons are the key to the editing power of PowerPoint. They allow you to replace the main Slide View edit window with an Outline View of the text which you can also edit. The Slide Sorter View displays thumbnail views of your work, and the Notes Pages View displays the notes page containing your scripted comments. Finally, the Slide Show view allows you to see your work as an electronic presentation on screen.

Outline View:

In Outline View, your work displays the slide titles and main text in typical outline mode. It is the easiest way of organising and editing presentation text.

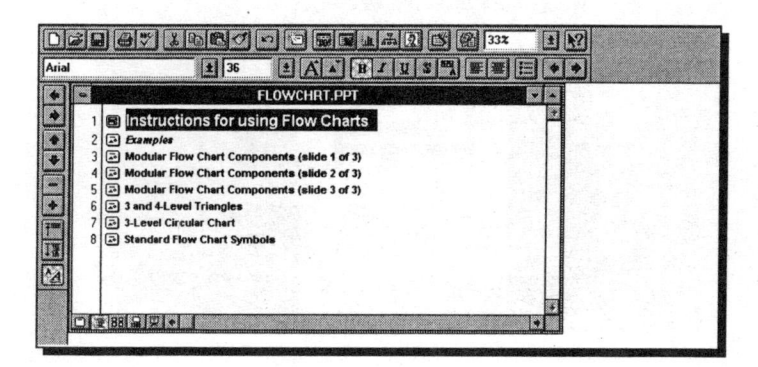

FLOWCHRT.PPT

1. Instructions for using Flow Charts
2. Examples
3. Modular Flow Chart Components (slide 1 of 3)
4. Modular Flow Chart Components (slide 2 of 3)
5. Modular Flow Chart Components (slide 3 of 3)
6. 3 and 4-Level Triangles
7. 3-Level Circular Chart
8. Standard Flow Chart Symbols

Slide Sorter View:

In this view, you can see the whole presentation at once. You can reorder slides, add transitions, and set timing for electronic presentations.

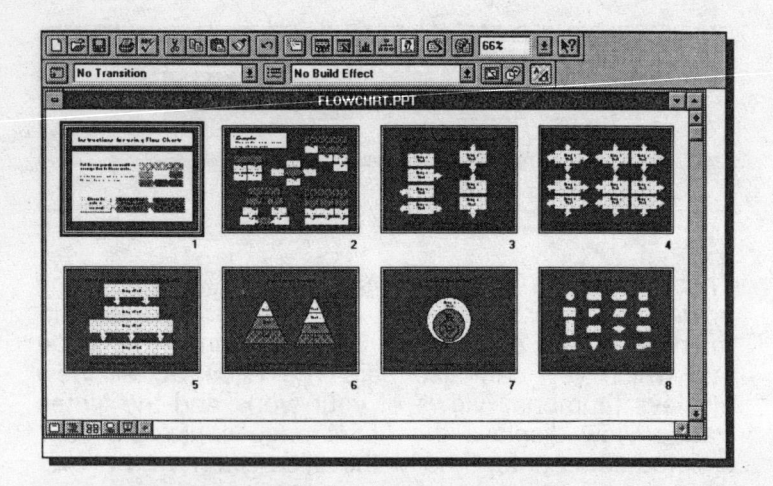

Notes Pages View:

This is where you create speaker's notes for any or all of your presentation slides.

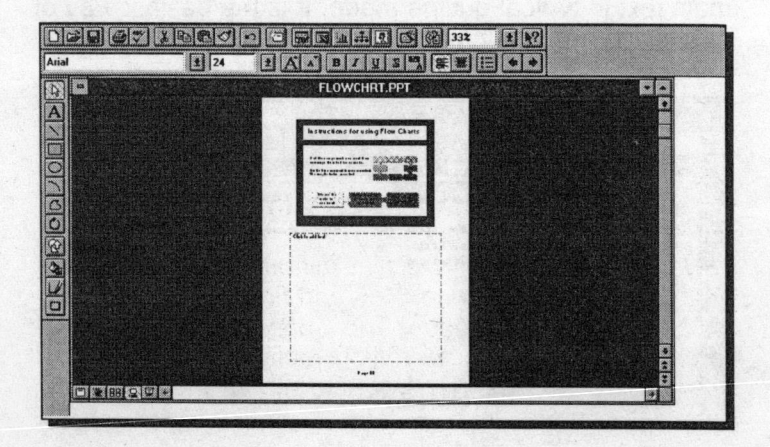

Slide Show View:

In this view you see your work as an electronic presentation, with each slide filling the screen. You can also see the effect of the transitions and timing that you set in the Slide Sorter View.

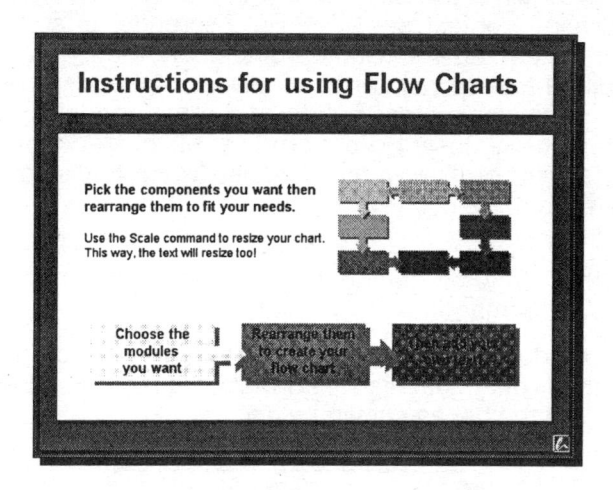

Instructions for using Flow Charts

Pick the components you want then rearrange them to fit your needs.

Use the Scale command to resize your chart. This way, the text will resize too!

Choose the modules you want

Rearrange them to create your flow chart

To see the next slide in full-screen view click the left mouse button. To return to a previous PowerPoint view from a full-screen Slide Show View, press <Esc>.

Also note that the Draw Toolbar is sometimes different in different PowerPoint views. Their function is easy to learn; just point to each unfamiliar button in turn and a ToolTip will appear in a yellow box.

Getting Familiar with PowerPoint

PowerPoint comes with a five-minute presentation on what the program can do. You can find **Quick Preview** under the **Help** menu. This preview is a good introduction to the powerful Templates and Wizards which Microsoft has incorporated into all the programs within MS-Office.

Using Help in PowerPoint

The Microsoft PowerPoint Help Program provides a comprehensive on-line help in exactly the same way as the Word and Excel Help programs. No matter what you are doing, you can either press the **F1** function key to display context sensitive Help screens, or click the Help button on the Standard toolbar, then move the modified mouse pointer to an area of the screen or on to a particular toolbar button and press the left mouse button, or choose **Help** from the Main Menu bar, to display a short menu, then choose **Index** to display the PowerPoint Help index.

Another way of getting help is with the **Help, Cue Cards** command.

Cue cards can also be used as a familiarisation option as they offer detailed information on a number of selected topics, as shown below.

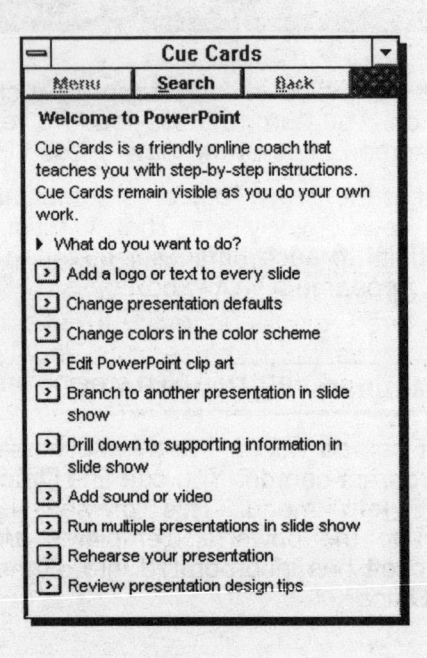

```
┌─────────────────────────────────────────┐
│  —            Cue Cards              ▼  │
├─────────────────────────────────────────┤
│   Menu      Search       Back           │
├─────────────────────────────────────────┤
│  Welcome to PowerPoint                  │
│                                         │
│  Cue Cards is a friendly online coach that │
│  teaches you with step-by-step instructions. │
│  Cue Cards remain visible as you do your own │
│  work.                                  │
│                                         │
│  ▶ What do you want to do?              │
│                                         │
│  [>] Add a logo or text to every slide  │
│  [>] Change presentation defaults       │
│  [>] Change colors in the color scheme  │
│  [>] Edit PowerPoint clip art           │
│  [>] Branch to another presentation in slide │
│      show                               │
│  [>] Drill down to supporting information in │
│      slide show                         │
│  [>] Add sound or video                 │
│  [>] Run multiple presentations in slide show │
│  [>] Rehearse your presentation         │
│  [>] Review presentation design tips    │
└─────────────────────────────────────────┘
```

11. DESIGNING A PRESENTATION

In this chapter we will use PowerPoint's Wizards to design a simple presentation quickly and effectively. Below, we show the first page of the finished presentation in black and white overhead format, so that you can have an idea of the overall design.

The AutoContent Wizard

When you first start PowerPoint, or you click the New icon on the Toolbar, shown here, you are offered the opportunity to use one of the Wizards, select a template on which to base your work, or begin with a blank presentation.

Most users would, without question, like to produce a presentation in no time at all. Wizards are an excellent starting point, even if you know what you want to do and how to do it. Therefore, select the **AutoContent Wizard** in the displayed New or PowerPoint dialogue box, discussed on page 121.

Later you can customise your presentation using PowerPoint's editing tools.

Clicking the **OK** button, starts the display of four dialogue boxes in which you are:

- Welcomed to the PowerPoint Wizards.
- Asked to specify what you are going to talk about (we typed the text *PowerPoint - The Wizards*).
- Asked to select the type of presentation you are going to give (we selected *Training*).
- Informed that your presentation is ready, and that you can replace suggested items at will.

The second and third dialogue boxes are displayed below.

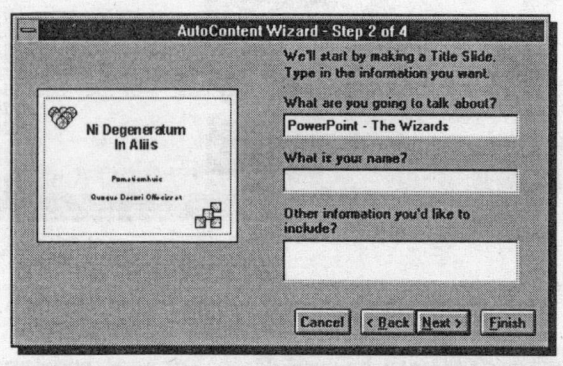

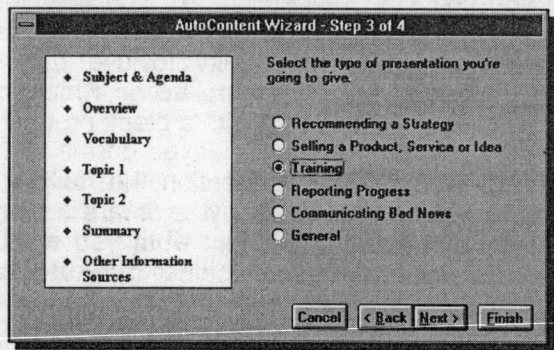

When you click the **Finish** button of the 4th dialogue box, the AutoContent Wizard displays the following suggested list of topics in Outline mode.

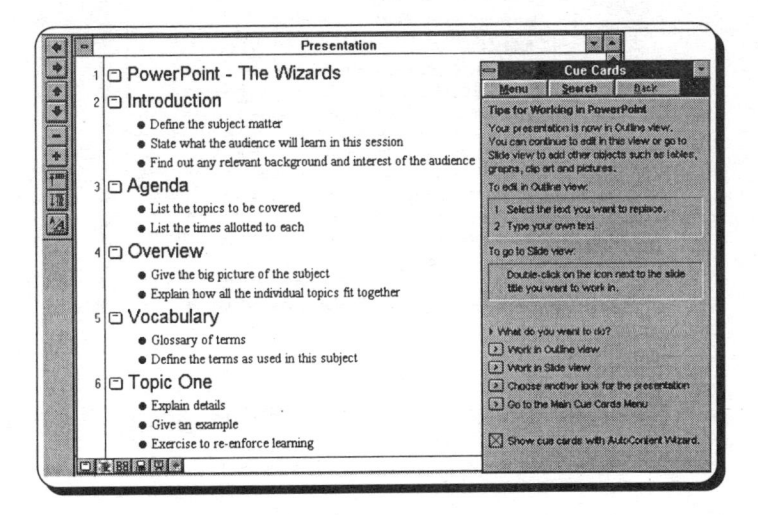

We have used the usual editing methods (see Chapter 4) to replaced some of the suggested topics with our own, added some extra demoted (more indented) topics using the Demote button on the Outline Toolbar, shown here, and deleted topics that were of no relevance to our presentation.

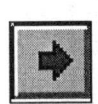

To return to the original bulleted level from a demoted level, you will have to use the Promote button on the Outline Toolbar.

The result of our efforts is displayed on the next page. Note that each numbered topic in the Outline mode, results in a different slide. These can be viewed by clicking the double arrow buttons at the extreme bottom right part of the window - see lower screen display on next page.

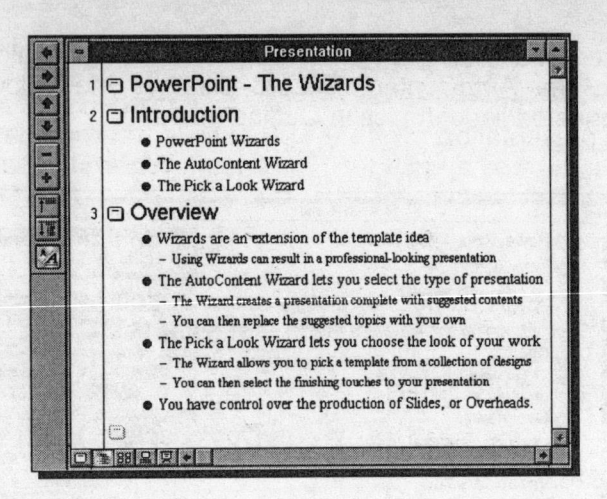

```
┌─────────────────────────────────────────┐
│              Presentation               │
├─────────────────────────────────────────┤
│  1 □ PowerPoint - The Wizards           │
│  2 □ Introduction                       │
│       ● PowerPoint Wizards              │
│       ● The AutoContent Wizard          │
│       ● The Pick a Look Wizard          │
│  3 □ Overview                           │
│       ● Wizards are an extension of the template idea │
│         - Using Wizards can result in a professional-looking presentation │
│       ● The AutoContent Wizard lets you select the type of presentation │
│         - The Wizard creates a presentation complete with suggested contents │
│         - You can then replace the suggested topics with your own │
│       ● The Pick a Look Wizard lets you choose the look of your work │
│         - The Wizard allows you to pick a template from a collection of designs │
│         - You can then select the finishing touches to your presentation │
│       ● You have control over the production of Slides, or Overheads. │
└─────────────────────────────────────────┘
```

Moving the insertion pointer within the text of slide 1 and clicking the Slide View button at the bottom of the screen, displays the following screen:

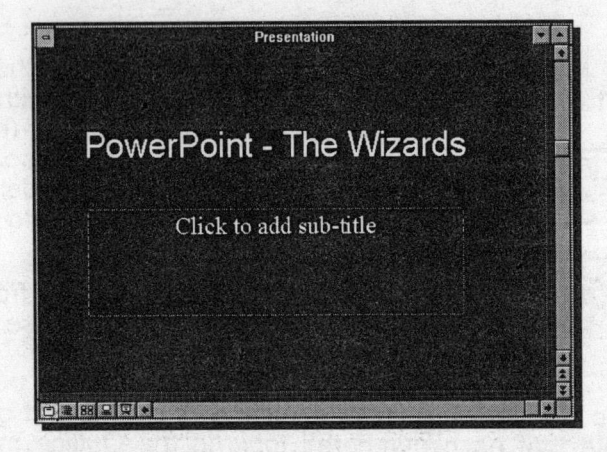

```
┌─────────────────────────────────────────┐
│              Presentation               │
├─────────────────────────────────────────┤
│                                         │
│                                         │
│      PowerPoint - The Wizards           │
│                                         │
│      ┌───────────────────────────┐      │
│      │   Click to add sub-title  │      │
│      │                           │      │
│      └───────────────────────────┘      │
│                                         │
└─────────────────────────────────────────┘
```

First, click within the dotted area of the first slide of your presentation and add the sub-title *One step at a time*. Next, save your work as **present1**, using the **File, Save As** command.

The Pick a Look Wizard

Our presentation might not be exactly what we had in mind, but we can use the Pick a Look Wizard to change the overall design.

To change the default design of slides, do the following:

- Click the Pick a Look Wizard button on PowerPoint's toolbar, shown here, which displays 9 dialogue boxes, one after the other.
- On the second dialogue box, select Black and White Overheads.
- On the third dialogue box, click the **More** button which opens the Presentation Template dialogue box, shown below.

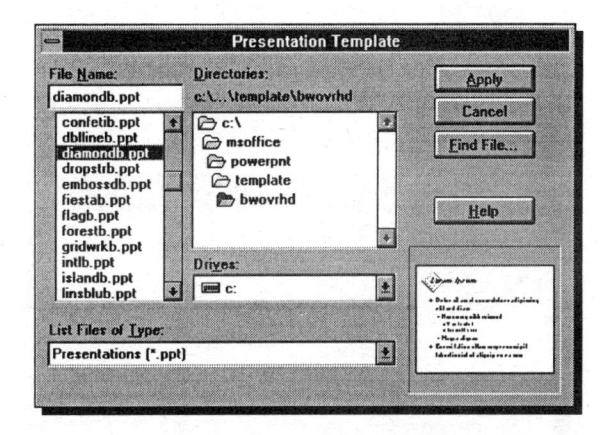

- In the Presentation Template dialogue box, select the **diamondb.ppt** file, and click the **Apply** button.
- Either look at the rest of the dialogue boxes and accept the default options, or click the **Finish** button on the third dialogue box.

The result, so far, is saved under the filename **present2**. We chose to display our work as a Black and White Overhead, as this prints better on the page. However, if you are fond of colour, you could choose On-Screen Presentation instead.

Below, we show the process of moving the main title from its present position to the position shown by the dotted rectangles. To achieve this, do the following:

- Point within the text area of the title and click the left mouse button. This causes a border to appear around the title.
- Place the mouse pointer on the title border and click the left mouse button. This places handles around the border, which can be used to increase the size of the border.
- To move the title, place the mouse pointer on the title border and drag it to the new position. The outer dotted rectangle indicates the border, while the inner dotted rectangle indicates the position of the text.

Inserting a Clip Art Image

To personalise our work, let us insert a clip art image on the front page of our presentation. To do this, click the Insert Clip Art button on the Toolbar, shown here. This opens the Microsoft ClipArt Gallery, provided you have the means of accessing it, from which you can choose a picture.

Usually, the ClipArt Gallery is held on a CD-ROM disc because of its size. Note the different categories; there are 33 in all, each one of which has at least 25 images. We chose the first image of the second row of the Academic category.

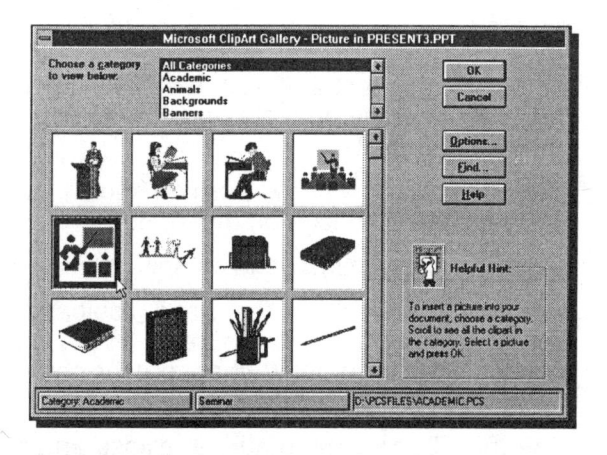

Clicking the **OK** button, transfers the image onto the title page of our presentation.

If you do not have access to the Microsoft ClipArt Gallery, you could always draw your own design.

Our final result (we will tell you what text enhancements to apply and what additional text to insert using the Draw Toolbar), is shown overleaf.

To obtain the design shown above, do the following:

- Select the title text and click the Bold icon on the Tool bar. The title appears in italics as part of our choice of template.
- Move the sub-title to the position shown, select it and click the Bold icon on the Toolbar.
- Move the Clip Art image to its new position.
- Use the Text Tool on the Draw Toolbar to add text at the bottom of the screen. We chose the letters *CSM* - you could choose your company's name or even your initials.
- Use the Ellipse Tool to add an ellipse around the typed letters.

Save the final presentation under the name **present3**.

* * *

PowerPoint is obviously capable of a lot more than we have introduced here, but you should now have the confidence to explore more of the package by yourself.

12. THE ACCESS DATABASE

Microsoft Access is a database management system (DBMS) designed to allow users to store and retrieve information easily and quickly. A database is a collection of data that exists and is organised around a specific theme or requirement. It can be of the 'flat-file' type, or it can have relational capabilities, as in the case of Access, which is known as a relational database management system (RDBMS).

The main difference between flat-file and relational database systems is that the latter can store and manipulate data in multiple 'tables', while the former systems can only manipulate a single table at any given time. To make accessing the data easier, each row (or **record**) of data within a database table is structured in the same fashion, i.e., each record will have the same number of columns (or **fields**).

We define a database and its various elements as follows:

Database	A collection of data organised for a specific theme in one or more tables.
Table	A two-dimensional structure in which data is stored, like in a spreadsheet
Record	A row of information in a table relating to a single entry and comprising one or more fields.
Field	A single column of information of the same type, such as people's names.

In Access the maximum number of tables in a database is limited to 128 and the maximum number of fields in a table to 256. However, the maximum number of records in a table is limited only by the capacity of your system.

A good example of a flat-file database is the invoicing details kept on clients by a company. These details could include name of client, description of work done, invoice number, and amount charged, as follows:

NAME	Consultancy	Invoice	Value
VORTEX Co. Ltd	Wind Tunnel Tests	9501	120.84
AVON Construction	Adhesive Tests	9502	103.52
BARROWS Associates	Tunnel Design Tests	9503	99.32
STONEAGE Ltd	Carbon Dating Tests	9504	55.98
PARKWAY Gravel	Material Size Tests	9505	180.22
WESTWOOD Ltd	Load Bearing Tests	9506	68.52

Such a flat-file DBMS is too limited for the type of information normally held by most companies. If the same client asks for work to be carried out regularly, then the details for that client (which could include address, telephone and fax numbers, contact name, date of invoice, etc., will have to be entered several times. This can lead to errors, but above all to redundant information being kept on a client - each entry will have to have the name of the client, their address, telephone and fax numbers.

The relational facilities offered by Access, overcome the problems of entry errors and duplication of information. The ability to handle multiple tables at any one time allows for the grouping of data into sensible subsets. For example, one table, called client, could hold the name of the client, their address, telephone and fax numbers, while another table, called invoice, could hold information on the work done, invoice number, date of issue, and amount charged. The two tables must have one unique common field, such as client reference number. The advantage is that details of each client are entered and stored only once, thus reducing the time and effort wasted on entering duplicate information, and also reducing the space required for data storage.

Starting Access

To start Access you need to first start Windows. When the program is loaded, open the Windows Program Manager, and if you are using a mouse, point to the Access icon, shown here, and double-click the left mouse button.

With the keyboard, after opening the Windows Program Manager, use the <Ctrl+Tab> key combination until the Microsoft Access Group is highlighted, then use the cursor keys to highlight the Access application icon, and press the <Enter> key.

The Welcome to Access Screen:

It is perhaps worth spending some time looking through the various parts of the MS Access Cue Cards that teach you about Microsoft Access.

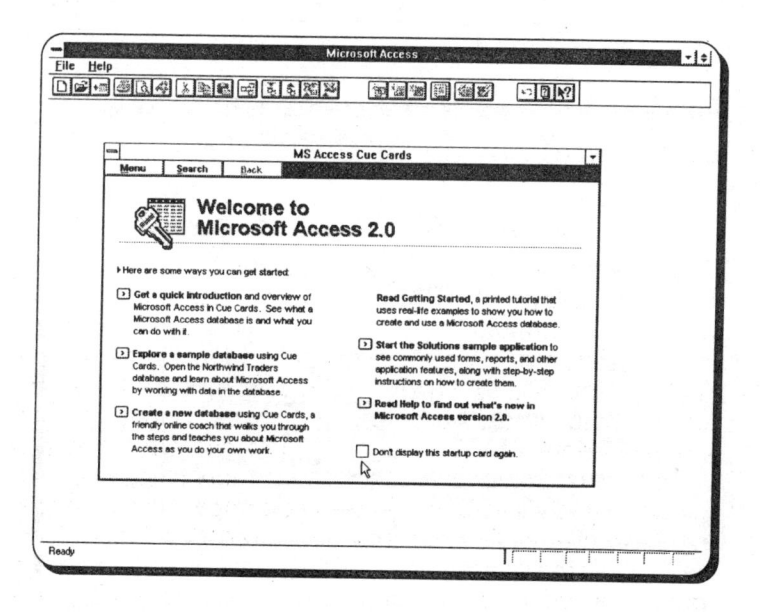

For example, to **Get a quick introduction** point to the first ▶ button and click the left mouse button. This opens up a new MS Access Cue Cards window with more options for you to choose from.

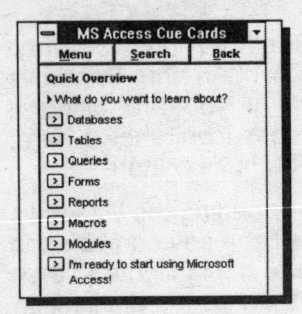

If you don't want the Cue Cards window to open next time you start Access, click at the small square at the bottom of the opening screen so that a large X appears in it.

Parts of the Access Screen

Below we show the Access opening screen with the MS Access Cue Cards application also displaying its welcoming screen.

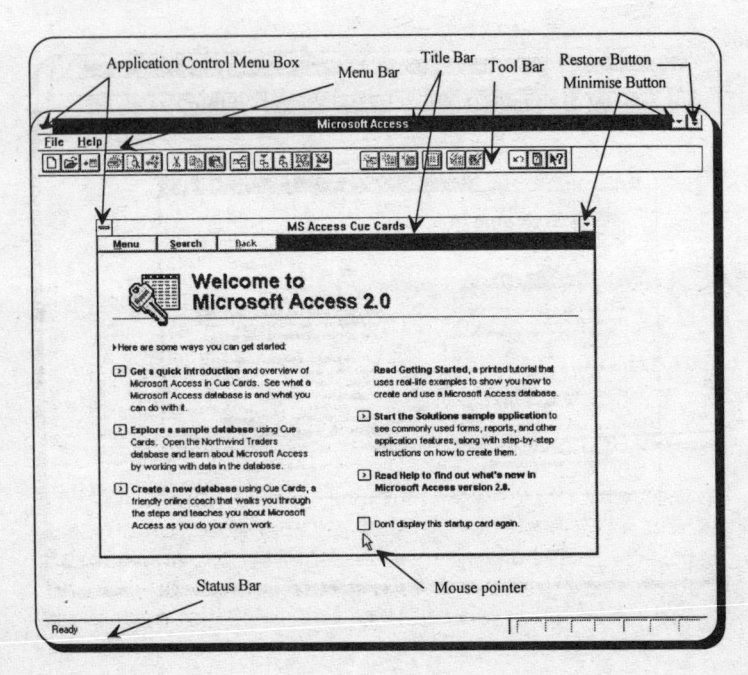

138

As you can see, these application and document windows have some common screen elements with those of other MS-Office applications. As usual, depending on what you are doing with Access, the items on the menu bar can be different from those of the opening screen. Also, although more than one window can be displayed simultaneously, only one is the active window which displays at the top of any other non-active windows (the exception being MS Access Cue Cards - to close it, press <Alt+F4>).

Using Help in Access

The Access Help Program functions in exactly the same way as the Help Program of the other MS-Office applications. No matter what you are doing, pressing the **F1** function key displays a help screen.

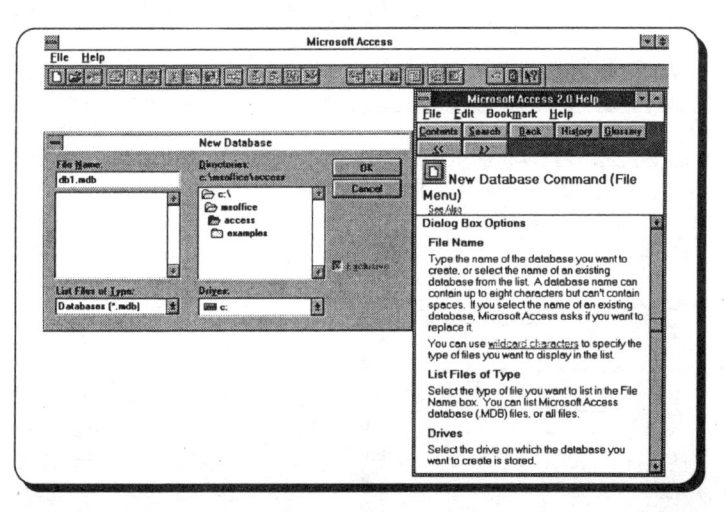

Another way of getting context sensitive help is to click the Help button on the Toolbar, shown here, then move the modified mouse pointer to an Access menu option or to a given Toolbar button and click the left mouse button. This opens an appropriate help screen.

Database Elements

To start designing a database using Microsoft Access, start Access, which opens the simple, two-menu option Access screen, with the **File** and **Help** options on the Menu bar. If the MS Access Cue Cards program loads, double-click the Application Control Menu Box, to close this application.

Next click the New Database icon, shown to the left, or use the **File, New Database** command, which causes the New Database dialogue box to be displayed, as follows:

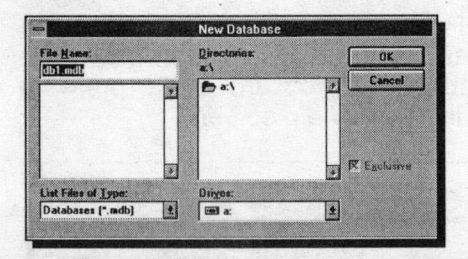

In the **File Name** box, type the database name, say Adept1, the program will insert automatically the **.mdb** extension. To avoid creating this database in the \ACCESS directory (the default directory chosen by Access), either select the \SAMAPPS subdirectory, or a working directory of your choice. We decided to save this example on a floppy disc, therefore we clicked the down arrow against the **Drives** box, and selected the A: drive.

On pressing the **OK** button, the Database window, shown to the left, opens. It is from here that you can design the various elements that make up a database, such as Tables, Queries, Forms, and Reports.

140

13. CREATING A TABLE

To design a database table, click the **New** button, which displays the New Table, shown below to the right of the Database window, with the two large buttons **Table Wizards** and **New Table**. The first allows you to automatically select from a list of pre-defined table applications, while the second allows you to start designing a table from scratch.

Clicking the **Table Wizards** button, opens the dialogue box shown at the lower right corner of the composite screen dump below.

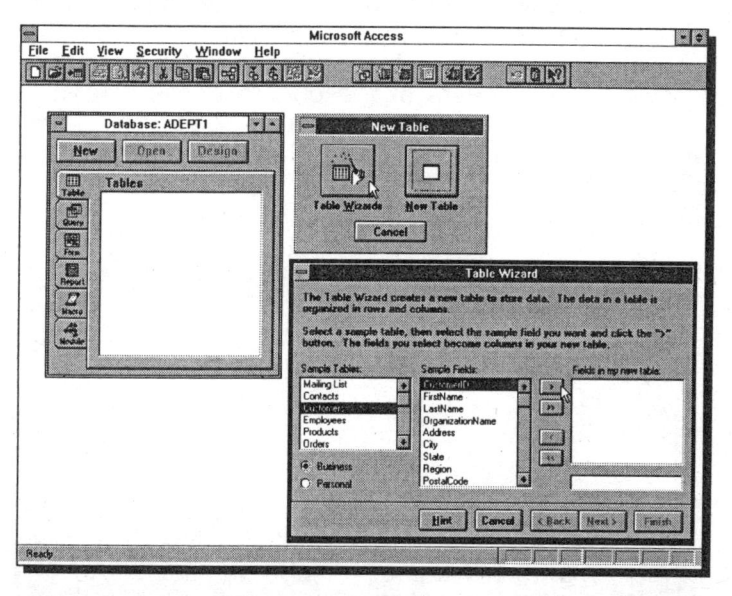

The database we are going to create holds the invoicing details which the firm Adept Consultants keep on their clients. One table will hold the details of the clients, while another will hold the actual invoice details. Choose 'Customers' from the **Sample Tables** list of the Table Wizard dialogue box, to reveal a list of appropriate fields for that table.

You can either select all the fields or you can select a few. For our example, we selected the following fields: CustomerID, OrganizationName, Address, City, Region, PostalCode, ContactName, PhoneNumber and FaxNumber, by highlighting each in turn and pressing the ▸ button.

Don't worry if these field names are not exactly what you want, as they can be changed easily. When you have selected all the required field names, press the **Finish** button, which displays the Customers Table ready for you to enter information.

To redesign the table, including changing its field names, click the Design View icon, or use the **View, Table Design** command, and edit the Field Name entries to those shown below. As each field name is highlighted, a Field Properties box appears at the bottom of the screen, in which you should also edit the name appearing against the Field Caption, or remove it altogether.

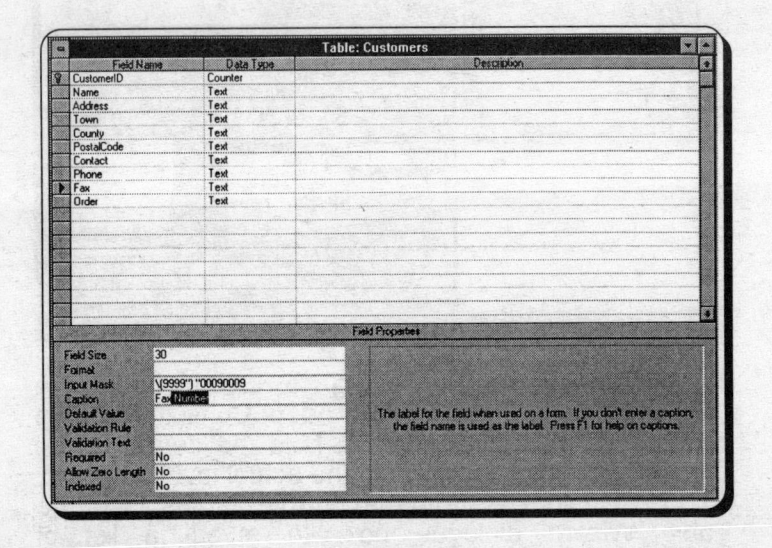

Next, place the cursor at the end of the Data Type descriptor of the CustomerID field which causes a down-arrow button to be displayed. Clicking this button, displays a drop-down list of data types, as shown here.

As we intend to use the first four letters of a company's name as the CustomerID field, change the current data type from Counter to Text.

Finally, first click the Save icon (or use the **File, Save** command) to save your design changes, then click the Datasheet View icon (or use the **View, Datasheet** command) to revert to the Customers table so that you can start entering information, as shown below.

Customer ID	Name	Address	Town	County	Post Code	Contact
VORT	VORTEX Co. Ltd	Windy House	St. Austell	Cornwall	TR18 1FX	Brian Storm
AVON	AVON Construction	Riverside House	Stratford-on-Avon	Warwickshire	AV15 2QW	John Waters
BARR	BARROWS Associates	Barrows House	Bodmin	Cornwall	PL22 1XE	Mandy Brown
STON	STONEAGE Ltd	Data House	Salisbury	Wiltshire	SB44 1BN	Mike Irons
PARK	PARKWAY Gravel	Aggregate House	Bristol	Avon	BS55 2ZX	James Stone
WEST	WESTWOOD Ltd	Weight House	Plymouth	Devon	PL22 1AA	Mary Slim
GLOW	GLOWORM Ltd	Light House	Brighton	Sussex	BR87 4DD	Peter Summers
SILV	SILVERSMITH Co	Radiation House	Exeter	Devon	EX28 1PL	Adam Smith
WORM	WORMGLAZE Ltd	Glass House	Winchester	Hampshire	WN23 5TR	Richard Glazer
EALI	EALING Engines Design	Engine House	Taunton	Somerset	TN17 3RT	Trevor Miles
HIRE	HIRE Service Equipment	Network House	Bath	Avon	BA76 3WE	Nicole Webb
EURO	EUROBASE Co. Ltd	Control House	Penzance	Cornwall	TR15 8LK	Sarah Star

The widths of the above fields were changed so that all fields could be visible on the screen at the same time. To change the width of a field, place the cursor on the column separator until the cursor changes to the vertical split arrow, then drag the column separator to the right or left, to increase or decrease the width of the field.

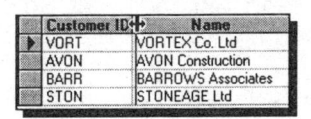

Sorting a Database Table

As you enter information into a database table, you might elect to change the field headings by clicking the Design Table icon and editing the Field Name entries. If you do this, on return to the Customers table you will find that the records have sorted automatically in ascending order of the entries of the field in which you left the cursor while in the Design Table.

Contact	Phone	Fax	Order
Brian Storm	01776-223344	01776-224466	1
John Waters	01657-113355	01657-221133	2
Mandy Brown	01554-664422	01554-663311	3
Mike Irons	01765-234567	01765-232332	4
James Stone	01534-987654	01534-984567	5
Mary Slim	01234-667755	01234-669988	6
Peter Summers	01432-746523	01432-742266	7
Adam Smith	01336-997755	01336-996644	8
Richard Glazer	01123-654321	01123-651234	9
Trevor Miles	01336-010107	01336-010109	10
Nicole Webb	01875-558822	01875-552288	11
Sarah Star	01736-098765	01736-098567	12
			Counter

If you want to preserve the order in which you entered your data, then add an Order field as the last field of your database table, and select its data type as Counter. This can be done at any time, even after you finished entering all other information in your table.

Sorting a database table in ascending order of a Counter type field, results in the database table displaying in the order in which the data was originally entered in that table. Above, we show the Contact field, so that you can cross-check the original order of your Customer table, as well as the rest of the information in that table not shown in the screen dump of the previous page.

To sort a database table in ascending or descending order of the entries of any field, place the cursor in the required field and click the Sort Ascending or Sort Descending icon, shown here.

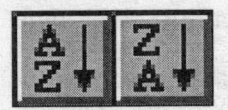

With the keyboard, select the **Records, Quick Sort** command, then choose either the **Ascending** or the **Descending** option.

Applying a Filter to a Sort:

If you would like to sort and display only records that fit selected criteria, then click the Edit Filter/Sort icon, shown here, or use the **Records, Edit Filter/Sort** command, which opens the Filter dialogue box, shown below.

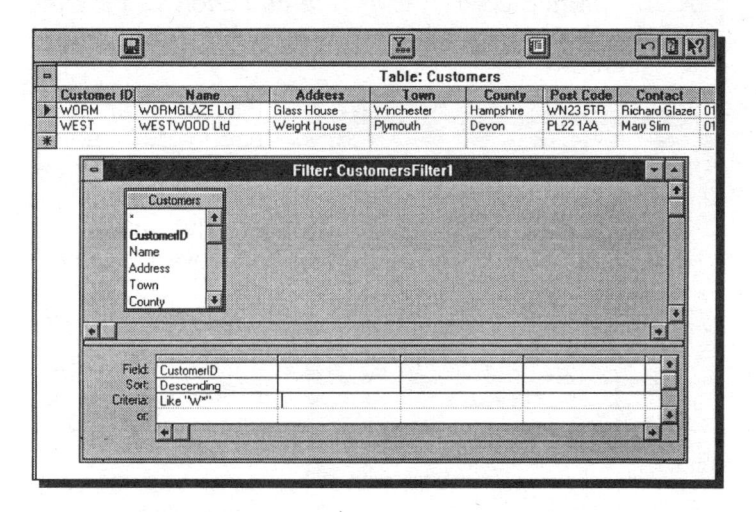

The upper portion of the dialogue box displays all the fields in the Customers table, while the lower portion is where you enter your filter restrictions. In the above example, we chose to view, in ascending order, the records within the CustomersID field that start with W - we typed W* and Access displayed *Like "W*"*.

On pressing the Filter Sort icon (shown here top left), the Customers table displays with only two entries, as seen in the above composite screen dump. To revert to the display of all the records, press the Show All Records icon (shown here bottom left).

To obtain extensive help on the subject, including an Examples screen, use the Query Pointer on the Filter dialogue box, then select Sorting and Filtering Records, followed by Entering Criteria in a Query or Criteria.

Using a Database Form

Once a table has been selected from the Database window, clicking the AutoForm icon, shown here, or using the **View Form** command, automatically displays each record of that table in form view. The created form for the Customers table is shown below.

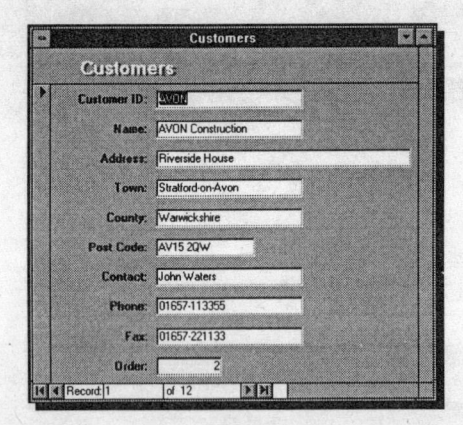

Forms can be used to enter, change or view data. They are mainly used to improve the way in which data is displayed on the screen.

Forms can also be used to sort records in a database table in ascending or descending order of a selected field.

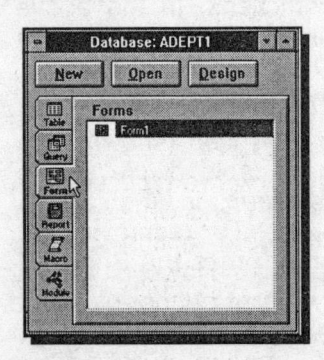

When you attempt to close a new Form window, you will be asked whether you would like to save it. An Access database can have lots of different forms, each designed with a different purpose in mind. Saved forms are displayed in the Database window when you press the Form button, as shown here.

In a later chapter we will discuss Form design in some detail, including their customisation.

Working with Data

Adding Records in a Table: Whether you are in Table view or Form view, to add a record, click the New icon, shown here.

When in Table view, the cursor jumps to the first empty record in the table (the one with the asterisk in the box to the left of the first field). When in Form view, Access displays an empty form which can be used to add a new record.

Finding Records in a Table: Whether you are in Table or Form view, to find a record click the Find icon, or use **Edit, Find**. This opens the following dialogue box:

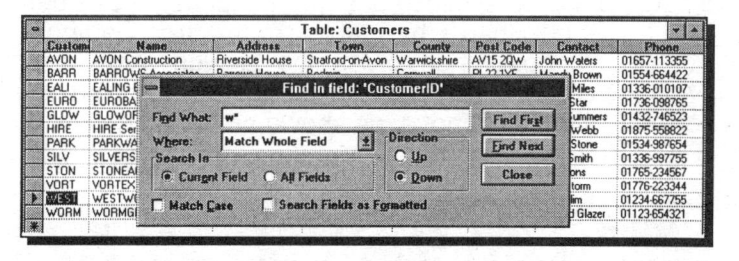

Note the field name on the Title bar, which is CustomerID, indicating that the cursor was on the CustomerID field before we clicked the Find icon or selected the **Find** command.

To find all the records starting with **w**, we type **w*** in the **Find What** box of the dialogue box and we search the **Current Field**. The **Current Field** option can be changed to **All Fields**, if you so wish. However, leaving it as it is and pressing the **Find First** button, highlights the first record with the CustomerID "WEST", as you can see from the composite screen dump above. Pressing the **Find Next** button, highlights the next record that matches our selected criteria.

Deleting Records from a Table: To delete a record when in Table view, point to the box to the left of the record to highlight the entire record, as shown below, then press the <Del> key.

| WEST | WESTWOOD Ltd | Weight House | Plymouth | Devon | PL22 1AA |
| WORM | WORMGLAZE Ltd | Glass House | Winchester | Hampshire | WN23 5TR |

To delete a record when in Form view, first display the record you want to delete, then use the **Edit, Select Record** command to select the whole record, and press the <Del> key.

In both cases you will be given a warning and you will be asked to confirm your decision.

Delete, Insert, and Move Fields in a Table: To delete a field from a table, close any forms that might be open, then load the table from the Database window, then press the Design View icon, click the row selector to highlight the field you want to remove, as shown below,

Table: Customers	
Field Name	Data Type
CustomerID	Text
Name	Text
Address	Text
Town	Text
County	Text
Post Code	Text

and press the Delete Row icon, shown here, or use the **Edit, Delete Row** command.

To insert a field in a table, display the table in Design View, and highlight the field above which you want to insert the new field, and press the Insert Row icon, shown here, or use the **Edit, Insert Row** command.

To move a field from its current to a new position in a table, select the field you want to move, then point to the row selector so that the mouse pointer is inclined as shown below, and drag the row to its new position.

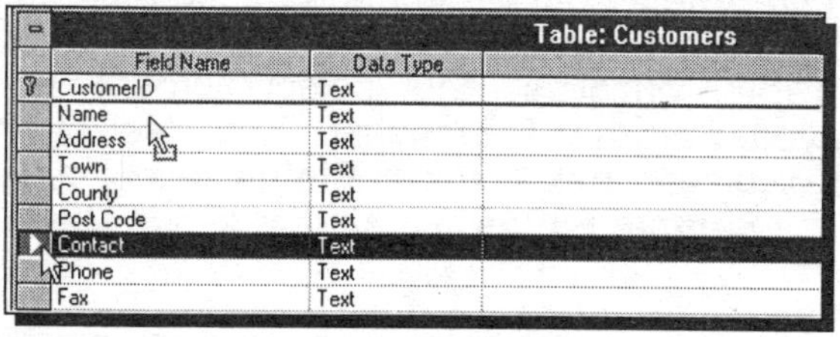

Field Name	Data Type
CustomerID	Text
Name	Text
Address	Text
Town	Text
County	Text
Post Code	Text
Contact	Text
Phone	Text
Fax	Text

Table: Customers

Note that while you are dragging the field, the mouse pointer changes to the one pointing at the Name field in the above composite. Releasing the mouse button, moves the Contact field to where the Name field is now and pushes all other fields one row down.

Printing a Table View:

You can print a database table by clicking the Print icon, or you can preview it on screen by clicking the Preview icon.

However, printing directly from here, produces a pre-defined print-out, the format of which you cannot control effectively. For example, the selected range in the Print dialogue box, must be contiguous. Also, even though you can choose to print in portrait or landscape by pressing the **S**etup button, you cannot control the printed font size.

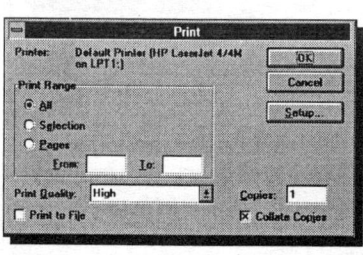

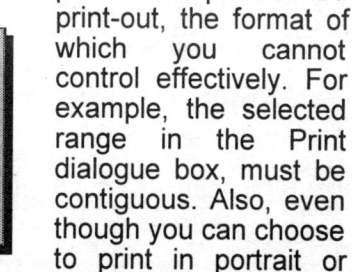

For a better method of producing a printed output, see the Report Design section.

Relational Database Design

In order to be able to discuss relational databases, we will add to the current database an Orders table.

Open the Adept1 database and use the **New** button on the Database window to add an Orders table to it. Use the **Table Wizards** and select Orders from the displayed **Sample Tables** list. Next, select the five fields displayed below under **Fields in my new table** from the **Sample Fields** list, and press the **Next** button.

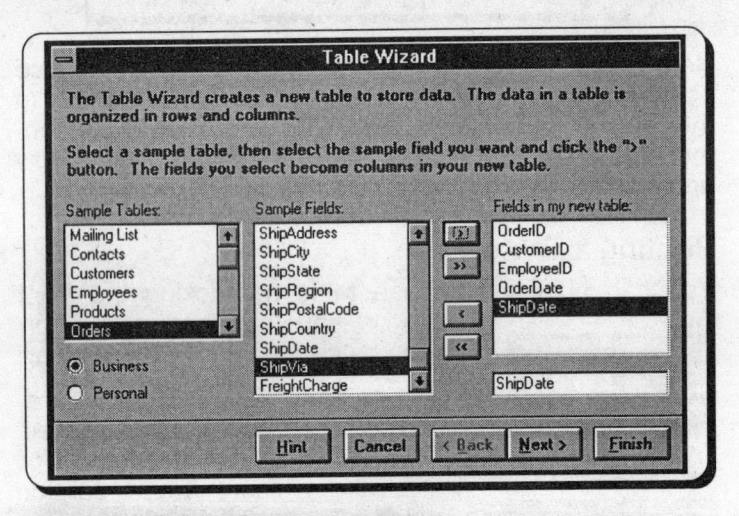

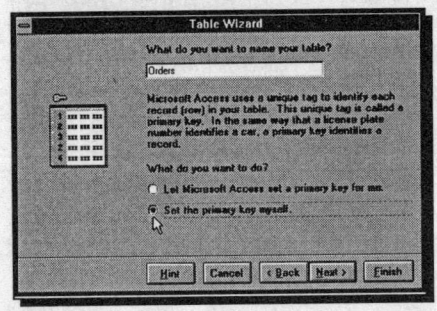

This displays the adjacent dialogue box in which you can, if you want to, change the name of the table.

Click the 'Set the primary key myself' option and press the **Next** button to select OrderID as the key field.

150

The key field must be unique in a table, and the OrderID field satisfies this requirement. This field is used by Access for fast searches.

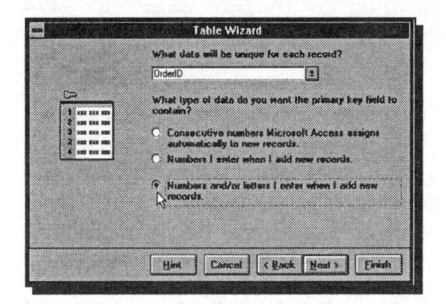

Now press the **Next** button and click the **Numbers and/or letters I enter when I add new records** option shown on the adjacent dialogue box. Finally, press the **Finish** button.

Next, use the Design Table facility, as discussed previously, to change the Data Types of the selected Field Names to those displayed below.

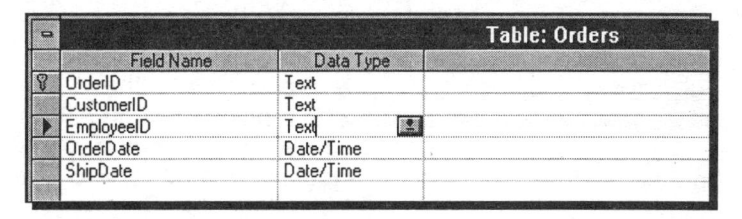

Field Name	Data Type
OrderID	Text
CustomerID	Text
EmployeeID	Text
OrderDate	Date/Time
ShipDate	Date/Time

The information you need to enter in the Orders table is shown below.

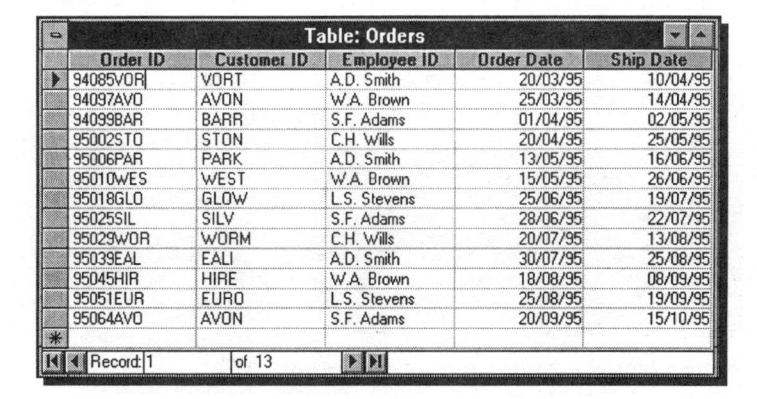

Order ID	Customer ID	Employee ID	Order Date	Ship Date
94085VOR	VORT	A.D. Smith	20/03/95	10/04/95
94097AVO	AVON	W.A. Brown	25/03/95	14/04/95
94099BAR	BARR	S.F. Adams	01/04/95	02/05/95
95002STO	STON	C.H. Wills	20/04/95	25/05/95
95006PAR	PARK	A.D. Smith	13/05/95	16/06/95
95010WES	WEST	W.A. Brown	15/05/95	26/06/95
95018GLO	GLOW	L.S. Stevens	25/06/95	19/07/95
95025SIL	SILV	S.F. Adams	28/06/95	22/07/95
95029WOR	WORM	C.H. Wills	20/07/95	13/08/95
95039EAL	EALI	A.D. Smith	30/07/95	25/08/95
95045HIR	HIRE	W.A. Brown	18/08/95	08/09/95
95051EUR	EURO	L.S. Stevens	25/08/95	19/09/95
95064AVO	AVON	S.F. Adams	20/09/95	15/10/95

Relationships

Information held in two or more tables of a database is normally related in some way. In our case, the two tables, Customers and Orders, are related by the CustomerID field.

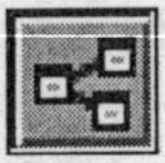

To build up relationships between tables, return to the Database window and press the Relationships icon on the Tool bar, shown here. This opens the following window in which the index field in each table is emboldened.

You can build relationships between tables by dragging a field name from one table into another. In our example, we have dragged CustomerID from the Customers table (by pointing to it, pressing the left mouse button, and while keeping the mouse button pressed, dragging the pointer) to the required field in the other table, in this case CustomerID in the Orders table. Releasing the mouse button opens the following dialogue boxes (the second one by pressing the **Join Type** button on the first one).

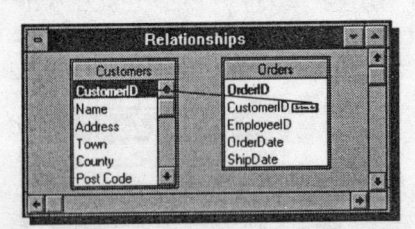

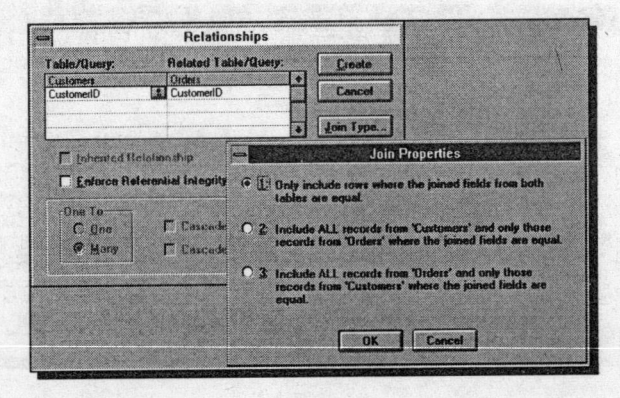

On the Join Properties dialogue box you can specify the type of join Access should create in new queries - more about this later. For the present, press the **OK** button on the Join Properties dialogue box, to close it, then check the **Enforce Referential Integrity** box in the Relationships dialogue box, and press the **Create** button. Access creates and displays graphically the chosen type of relationship in the Relationships window shown here. Note the relationship "1 customer to many (∞) orders" symbolism in the Relationships window.

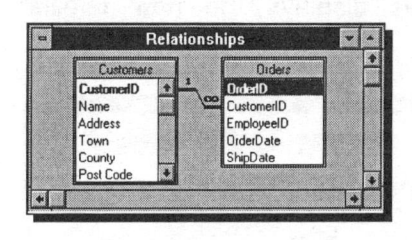

Because Access is a relational database, data can be used in queries from more than one table at a time. As we have seen, if the database contains tables with related data, the relationships can be defined easily. Usually, the matching fields have the same name, as in our example of Customers and Orders tables. In the Customers table, the CustomersID field is the primary field and relates to the CustomersID field in the Orders table - there can be several orders in the Orders table from one customer in the Customers table.

The various types of relationships are as follows:

- Inherited - for attaching tables from another Access database. The original relationships of the attached database can be used in the current database.

- Referential - for enforcing relationships between records according to certain rules, when you add or delete records in related tables belonging to the same database. For example, you can only add records to a related table, if a matching record already exists in the primary table, and you cannot delete a record from the primary table if matching records exist in a related table.

Viewing and Editing Relationships

To view the current relationships between tables in a database, activate the Database window and press the Relationships icon. This displays the now familiar Relationships window.

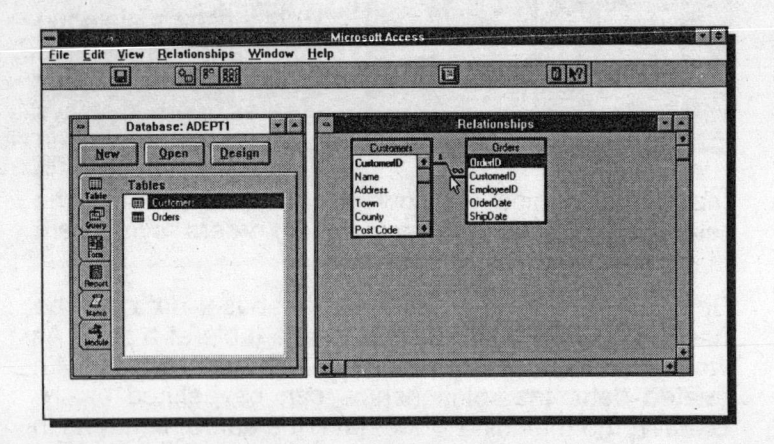

To edit a relationship, double-click the left mouse button at the position shown on the above screen dump. The tip of the mouse pointer must be on the inclined line joining the two tables in the Relationships window, as shown, before Access will respond. If you have difficulty with this action, first point to the relationship line and click once to embolden it, then use the **Relationships, Edit Relationship** command. Either of these two actions will open the Relationships dialogue box in which you can change the various options already discussed.

A given relationship can easily be removed altogether, by first activating it (pointing and clicking to embolden it), then pressing the <Del> key. A confirmation dialogue box will be displayed. To delete a table, you must first detach it from other tables, then select it in the Database Window and press the <Del> key. Think before you do this!

Creating an Additional Table

As an exercise, create a third table using the **Table Wizards** and select Invoices from the displayed **Sample Tables** list. Next, select the five fields displayed below - the names and their data types have been changed using the Design Table facility.

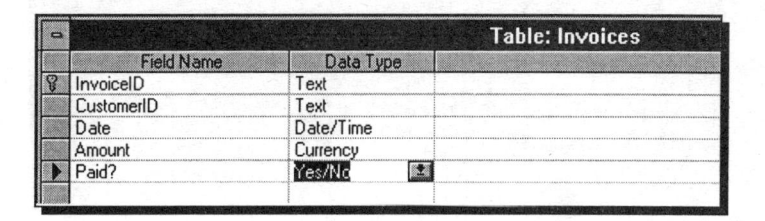

Table: Invoices

Field Name	Data Type
InvoiceID	Text
CustomerID	Text
Date	Date/Time
Amount	Currency
Paid?	Yes/No

Next, enter the data given below and build up appropriate relationships between the Invoices table, the Customers table and the Orders table, as shown overleaf.

Invoice No	Customer ID	Date	Amount	Paid?
AD9501	VORT	10/04/95	£120.84	No
AD9502	AVON	14/04/95	£103.52	Yes
AD9503	BARR	02/05/95	£99.32	No
AD9504	STON	25/05/95	£55.98	No
AD9505	PARK	16/06/95	£180.22	No
AD9506	WEST	26/06/95	£68.52	No
AD9507	GLOW	19/07/95	£111.56	No
AD9508	SILV	22/07/95	£123.45	Yes
AD9509	WORM	13/08/95	£35.87	No
AD9510	EALI	25/08/95	£58.95	No
AD9511	HIRE	08/09/95	£290.00	No
AD9512	EURO	19/09/95	£150.00	No
AD9513	AVON	15/10/95	£135.00	No

The relationships between the three tables should be arranged as follows:

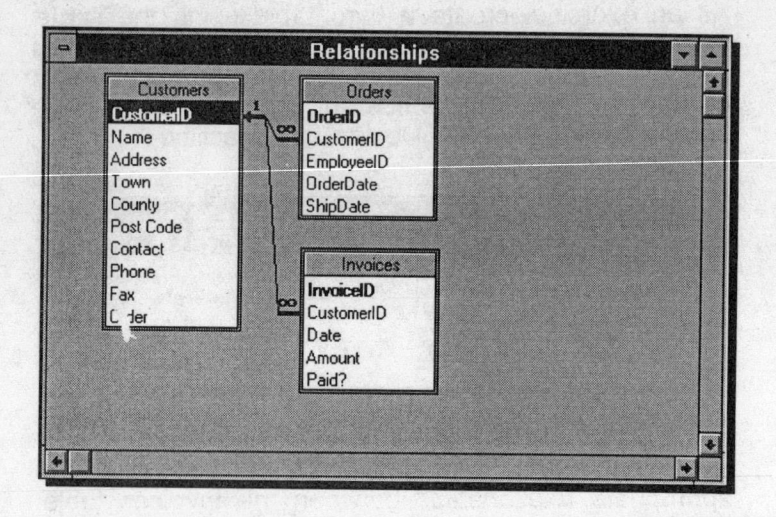

```
┌─ Relationships ─────────────────────────┐
│  ┌─Customers─┐    ┌─Orders────┐         │
│  │ CustomerID│─1─∞│ OrderID   │         │
│  │ Name      │    │ CustomerID│         │
│  │ Address   │    │ EmployeeID│         │
│  │ Town      │    │ OrderDate │         │
│  │ County    │    │ ShipDate  │         │
│  │ Post Code │    └───────────┘         │
│  │ Contact   │    ┌─Invoices──┐         │
│  │ Phone     │    │ InvoiceID │         │
│  │ Fax       │──∞│ CustomerID │         │
│  │ Order     │    │ Date      │         │
│  └───────────┘    │ Amount    │         │
│                   │ Paid?     │         │
│                   └───────────┘         │
└─────────────────────────────────────────┘
```

It is important that you should complete the above exercise, as it consolidates what we have done so far and, in any case, we will be using all three tables in what comes next.

14. CREATING A QUERY

You create a query so that you can ask questions about the data in your database tables. For example, you could find out whether you have more than one order from the same customer in our Adept database.

Before carrying on, use Windows' File Manager to copy **adept1.mdb** to **adept2.mdb**. We suggest you do this fairly frequently to make a backup of your database, in case a file gets corrupted. Next, start Access, load Adept1, and in the Database window click the **Query** button, followed by the **New** button which displays the New Query dialogue box.

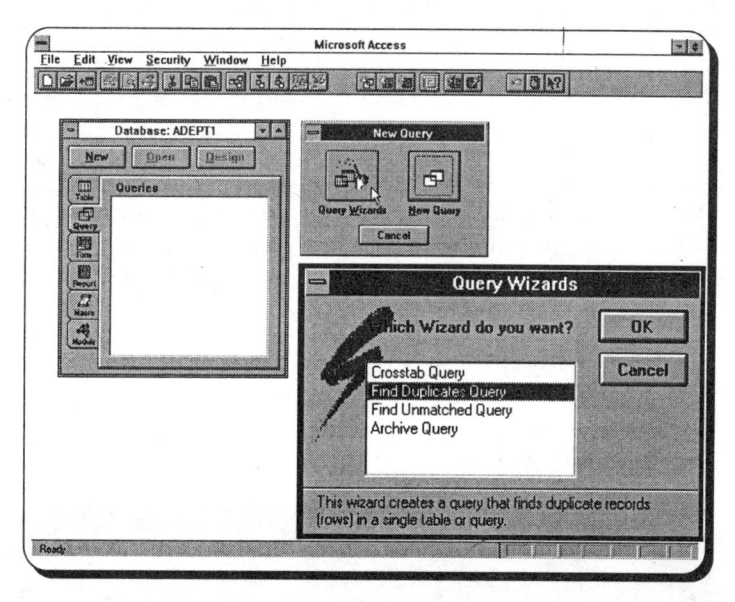

Next, click the **Query Wizards** button which opens the Query Wizards dialogue box, shown in the composite screen dump above, and select the **Find Duplicates Query** option. On clicking **OK**, the Find Duplicates Query Wizards dialogue box is displayed, as shown on the next page.

157

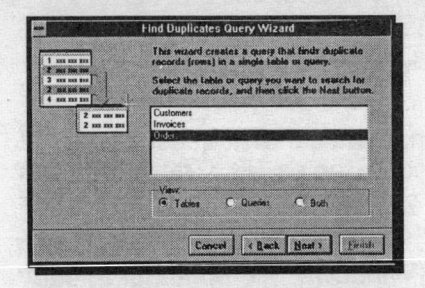

From the displayed database tables in this dialogue box, select the Orders table and press the **Next** button.

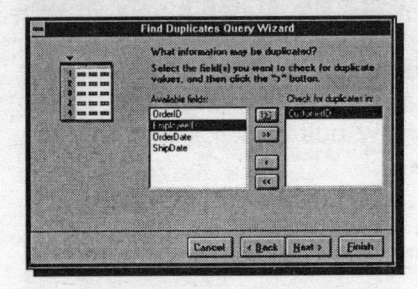

On the following dialogue box select **CustomerID** as the field you want to check for duplicate values, then press the 🔲 button, followed by the **Next** button.

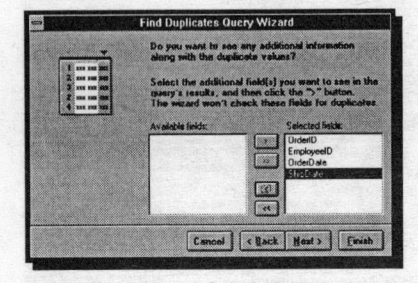

Finally, select the additional fields you would like to see along with the duplicate values, by selecting those you want from the next dialogue box, either one at a time or, if you decide to select all of them, as shown here, by clicking the 🔲 button. Clicking the **Finish** button displays the following Select Query screen.

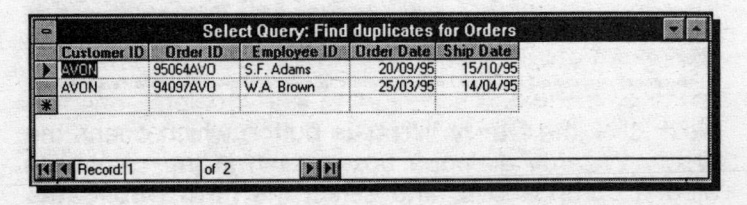

Customer ID	Order ID	Employee ID	Order Date	Ship Date
AVON	95064AVO	S.F. Adams	20/09/95	15/10/95
AVON	94097AVO	W.A. Brown	25/03/95	14/04/95

If you examine the original Orders table, you will indeed find that it contains two orders from AVON.

158

Types of Queries

The query we have created so far, is known as the *Select Query*, which is the most common type of query. However, with Access you can also create and use other types of queries, as follows:

- **Crosstab query** - used to present data with row and column headings, just like a spreadsheet. It can be used to summarise large amounts of data in a more readable form.

- **Action query** - used to make changes to many records in one operation. For example, you might like to remove from a given table all records that meet certain criteria, make a new table, or append records to a table. Obviously, this type of query has to be treated with care!

- **Union query** - used to match fields from two or more tables.

- **Pass-through query** - used to pass commands to an SQL (see below) database.

- **Data-definition query** - used to create, change, or delete tables in an Access database using SQL statements.

SQL stands for Structured Query Language, often used to query, update, and manage relational databases. Each query created by Access has an associated SQL statement that defines the action of that query. Thus, if you are familiar with SQL, you can use such statements to view and modify queries, or set form and report properties. However, these actions can be done more easily with the QBE (query-by-example) grid, to be discussed next. If you design union queries, pass-through queries, or data-definition queries, then you must use SQL statements, as these type of queries can not be designed with the QBE grid. Finally, to create a subquery, you use the QBE grid, but you enter an SQL SELECT statement for criteria, as we shall see in the next QBE grid example.

The Query Window

The Query window is a graphical query-by-example (QBE) tool. Because of Access' graphical features, you can use the mouse to select, drag, and manipulate objects in the query window to define how you would like to see your data.

An example of a ready made Query window can be seen by selecting the Find duplicates for Orders query and clicking the **Design** button on the Database window. This action opens the Select Query dialogue box shown below.

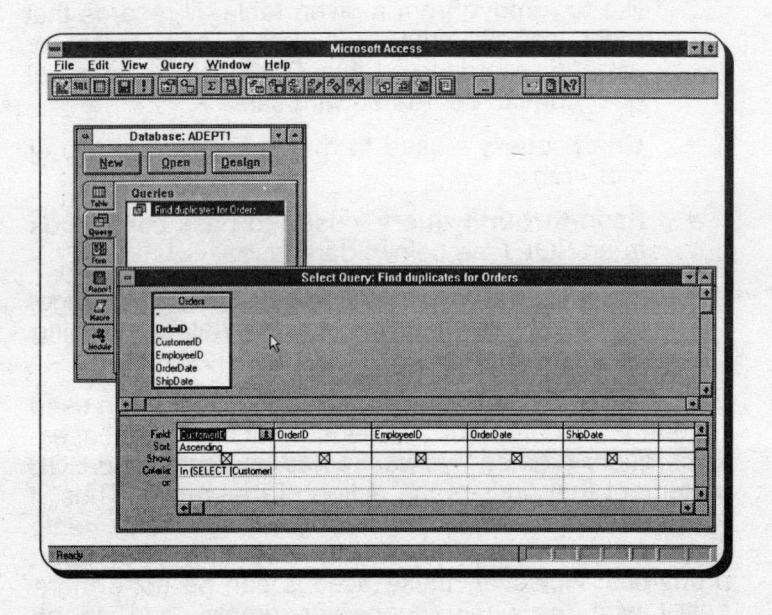

You can add a table to the top half of the Query window by simply dragging the table from the Database window. Similarly, you can add fields to the bottom half of the Query window (the QBE grid) by dragging fields from the tables on the top half of the Query window. In addition, the QBE grid is used to select the sort order of the data, or insert criteria, such as SQL statements.

To see the full SQL SELECT statement written by Access as the criteria selection when we first defined the query, widen the width of the first field, as follows:

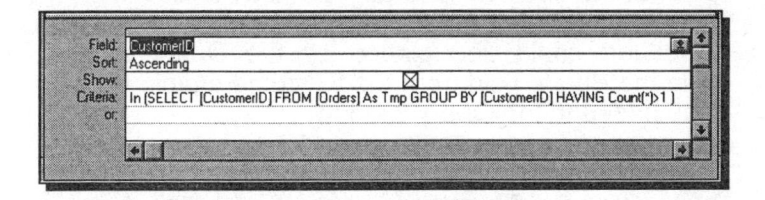

```
Field:    CustomerID
Sort:     Ascending
Show:             ☒
Criteria: In (SELECT [CustomerID] FROM [Orders] As Tmp GROUP BY [CustomerID] HAVING Count(*)>1 )
or:
```

Note the part of the statement which states 'As Tmp GROUP'. Access collects the data you want as a temporary group, called a *dynaset*. This special set of data behaves like a table, but it is not a table; it is a dynamic view of the data from one or more tables, selected and sorted by the particular query.

Creating a New Query:

Below, we show a composite screen created by clicking the **N**ew button on the Database window, then clicking the **New Query** button on the New Query dialogue box. This opens both the Select Query and the Add Table dialogue boxes. The Invoices and Customers tables were then added to the Select Query window.

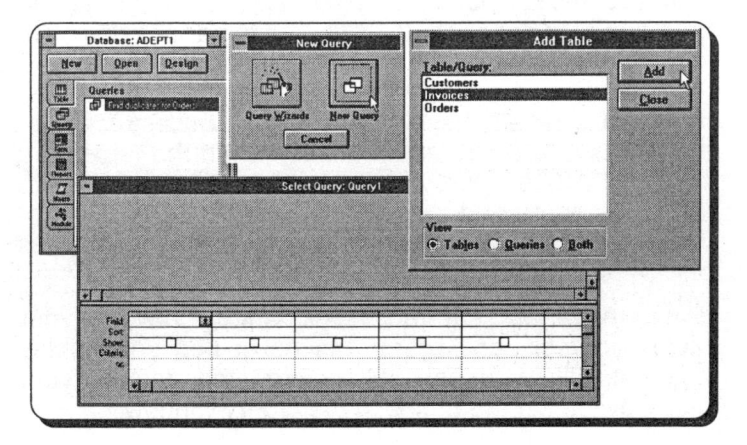

Adding Fields to a Query Window:

Below we show a screen in which the Paid? and InvoiceID fields have been dragged from the Invoices table and added to the Query window. In addition, the Name and Contact fields have been dragged from the Customers table and placed on the Query window, while the Phone field from the Customers table is about to be added to the Query window.

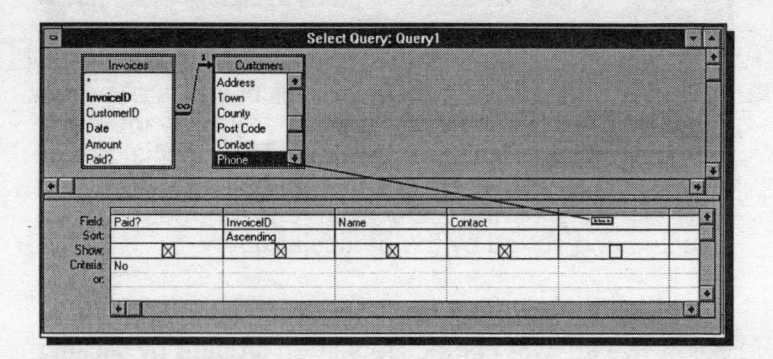

Having dragged all five fields from the two tables onto the QBE grid, we have added the word No as the criteria on the Paid? field and selected Ascending as the Sort for the InvoiceID field.

Note that the Invoices and Customers tables are joined by a line that connects the two CustomerID fields. The join line was created when we designed the tables and their relationships in the previous chapter. Even if you have not created these relationships, Access will join the tables in a query automatically when the tables are added to a query, provided each table has a field with the same name and a compatible data type and one of those fields is a primary key. A primary field is displayed in bold in the Query window.

If you have not created relationships between your tables yourself, or Access has not joined your tables automatically, you can still use related data in your query by joining the tables in the Query window.

Clicking the Run icon on the Tool bar, shown here, instantly displays all the unpaid invoices with the details you have asked for, as follows:

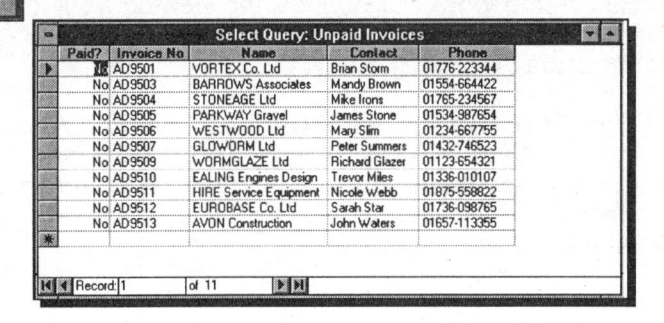

Paid?	Invoice No	Name	Contact	Phone
	AD9501	VORTEX Co. Ltd	Brian Storm	01776-223344
No	AD9503	BARROWS Associates	Mandy Brown	01554-664422
No	AD9504	STONEAGE Ltd	Mike Irons	01765-234567
No	AD9505	PARKWAY Gravel	James Stone	01534-987654
No	AD9506	WESTWOOD Ltd	Mary Slim	01234-667755
No	AD9507	GLOWORM Ltd	Peter Summers	01432-746523
No	AD9509	WORMGLAZE Ltd	Richard Glazer	01123-654321
No	AD9510	EALING Engines Design	Trevor Miles	01336-010107
No	AD9511	HIRE Service Equipment	Nicole Webb	01875-558822
No	AD9512	EUROBASE Co. Ltd	Sarah Star	01736-098765
No	AD9513	AVON Construction	John Waters	01657-113355

To save your newly created query, use the **File, Save Query As** command, and give it a name such as 'Unpaid Invoices'.

Types of Criteria:

Access accepts the following expressions as criteria:

Arithmetic Operators		Comparison Operators		Logical Operators	
*	Multiply	<	Less than	And	And
/	Divide	<=	Less than or equal	Or	Inclusive or
+	Add	>	Greater than	Xor	Exclusive or
-	Subtract	>=	Greater than or equal	Not	Not equivalent
		=	Equal	Eqv	Equivalent
		<>	Not equal	Imp	Implication

Other operators		
Between	Between 50 And 150	All values between 50 and 150
In	In("Bath","Bristol")	All records with Bath and Bristol
Is	Is Null	All records with no value in that field
Like	Like "Brian *"	All records with Brian something in field
&	[Name]&" "&[Surname]	Concatenates strings

Combining Criteria

By specifying additional criteria in a Query window you can create powerful queries for viewing your data. In the examples below we have added the field Amount to our Unpaid Invoices query.

The AND Criteria with Different Fields: When you insert criteria in several fields, but in the same row, Access assumes that you are searching for records that meet all of the criteria. For example, the criteria below list the following records:

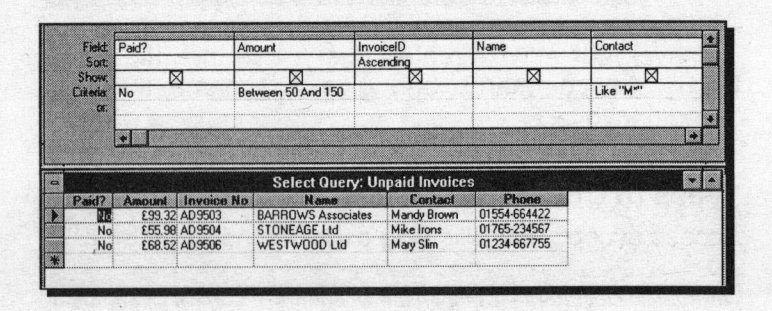

Field:	Paid?	Amount	InvoiceID	Name	Contact
Sort:			Ascending		
Show:	☒	☒	☒	☒	☒
Criteria:	No	Between 50 And 150			Like "M*"
or:					

Select Query: Unpaid Invoices

Paid?	Amount	Invoice No	Name	Contact	Phone
No	£99.32	AD9503	BARROWS Associates	Mandy Brown	01554-664422
No	£55.98	AD9504	STONEAGE Ltd	Mike Irons	01765-234567
No	£68.52	AD9506	WESTWOOD Ltd	Mary Slim	01234-667755

The OR Criteria with the Same Field: If you include multiple criteria in one field only, then Access assumes that you are searching for records that meet any one of the specified criteria. For example, the criteria <50 or >100 in the field Amount, shown below, list the required records, only if the No in the Paid? field is inserted in both rows.

Field:	Paid?	Amount	InvoiceID	Name	Contact
Sort:			Ascending		
Show:	☒	☒	☒	☒	☒
Criteria:	No	<50			
or:	No	>100			

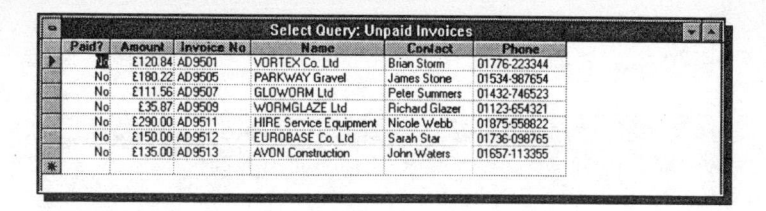

Paid?	Amount	Invoice No	Name	Contact	Phone
☒	£120.84	AD9501	VORTEX Co. Ltd	Brian Storm	01776-223344
No	£180.22	AD9505	PARKWAY Gravel	James Stone	01534-987654
No	£111.56	AD9507	GLOWORM Ltd	Peter Summers	01432-746523
No	£35.87	AD9509	WORMGLAZE Ltd	Richard Glazer	01123-654321
No	£290.00	AD9511	HIRE Service Equipment	Nicole Webb	01875-558822
No	£150.00	AD9512	EUROBASE Co. Ltd	Sarah Star	01736-098765
No	£135.00	AD9513	AVON Construction	John Waters	01657-113355

The OR Criteria with Different Fields: If you include multiple criteria in different fields, but in different rows, then Access assumes that you are searching for records that meet either one or the other of the specified criteria. For example, the criteria Yes in the Paid? field and the criteria <50 in the Amount field, but in different rows, list the following records.

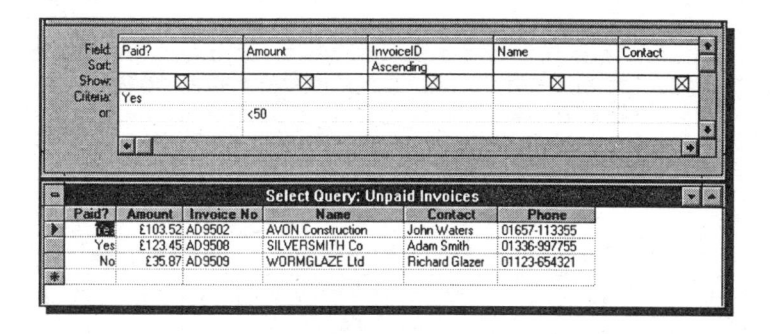

Field:	Paid?	Amount	InvoiceID	Name	Contact
Sort:			Ascending		
Show:	☒	☒	☒	☒	☒
Criteria:	Yes				
or:		<50			

Paid?	Amount	Invoice No	Name	Contact	Phone
Yes	£103.52	AD9502	AVON Construction	John Waters	01657-113355
Yes	£123.45	AD9508	SILVERSMITH Co	Adam Smith	01336-997755
No	£35.87	AD9509	WORMGLAZE Ltd	Richard Glazer	01123-654321

The AND and OR Criteria Together: The following choice of criteria will cause Access to retrieve either records that have Yes in the Paid? field and the company's name starts with the letter A, or records that the invoice amount is less than £50.

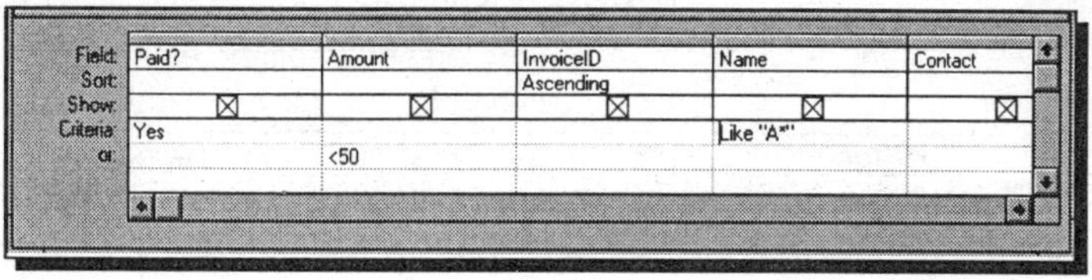

Field:	Paid?	Amount	InvoiceID	Name	Contact
Sort:			Ascending		
Show:	☒	☒	☒	☒	☒
Criteria:	Yes			Like "A*"	
or:		<50			

The retrieved records from such a query are shown below.

Paid?	Amount	Invoice No	Name	Contact	Phone
Yes	£103.52	AD9502	AVON Construction	John Waters	01657-113355
No	£35.87	AD9509	WORMGLAZE Ltd	Richard Glazer	01123-654321

Select Query: Unpaid Invoices

Using Wildcard Characters in Criteria:

In the previous example we used the criteria A* to mean any company whose name starts with the letter A. The asterisk in this criteria is known as a wildcard character.

To search for a pattern, you can use the asterisk (*) and the question mark (?) as wildcard characters when specifying criteria in expressions. An asterisk stands for any number of characters, while a question mark stands for any single character in the same position as the question mark.

The following examples show the use of wildcard characters in various types of expressions:

Entered Expression	Meaning	Examples
a?	Any two-letter word beginning with A	am, an, as, at
???d	Any four-letter word ending with d	find, hand, land, yard
Sm?th	Any five-letter word beginning with Sm and ending with th	Smith Smyth
fie*	Any word starting with the letters fie	field, fiend, fierce, fiery
*ght	Any word ending with ght	alight, eight, fight, light, might, sight
*/5/95	All dates in May '95	1/5/95

15. USING FORMS & REPORTS

You can use forms to find, edit, and add data in a convenient manner. Access provides you with an easy way of designing various types of forms, some of which are discussed here. Forms look good on screen, but do not produce very good output on paper, whereas reports are designed to look good on paper, but do not necessarily look good on screen.

Using the Form Wizards

Using the Form Wizards, you can easily display data from either a table or a query in form view.

In the Database window, first click on the Form button, then click the **New** button which opens the New Form dialogue box in which you must choose either a table or a query on which to base the new form. In the screen dump below, we have chosen the Invoices table.

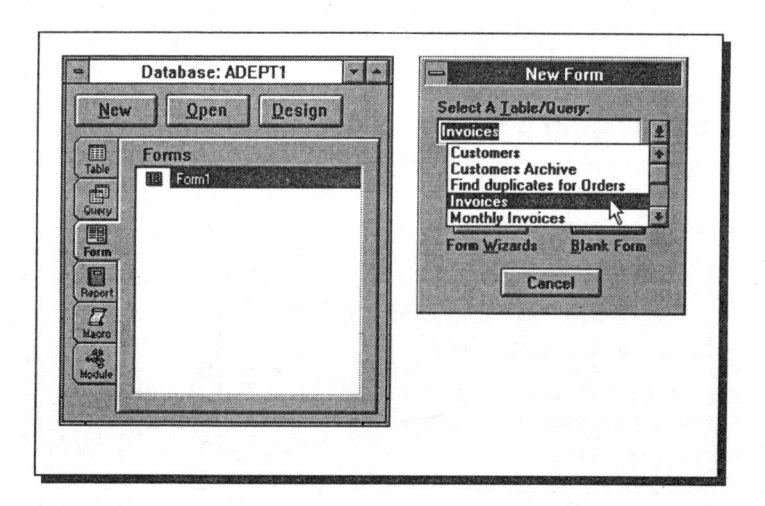

Next, click the **Form Wizards** button which displays the Form Wizards dialogue box, shown here. As you can see, there are five different types of forms available for you to choose from. The list below explains their function.

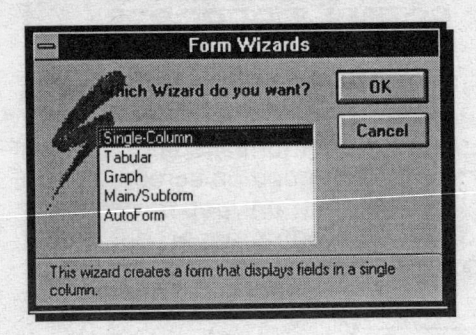

Type of Form	Function
Single-Column	Displays fields in a single column.
Tabular	Displays each record as a row of fields.
Graph	Displays data graphically.
Main/Subform	Displays a form that contains another form. This form allows data from related tables to be viewed at the same time.
AutoForm	Displays a simple form automatically.

Customising a Form:

You can customise a form by changing the appearance of text, data, and any other attributes. To have a look at some of these options, double click on Form1 to display the Customers form, then click the Design View button on the Tool bar. What appears on your screen is shown on the next page.

As you can see, a form in Design View is made up of boxes attached to a grid. Clicking at the County box, for example, causes markers to appear around it. When the mouse pointer is then placed within either the label box or data box, it changes to a hand which indicates that you can drag the box to a new position.

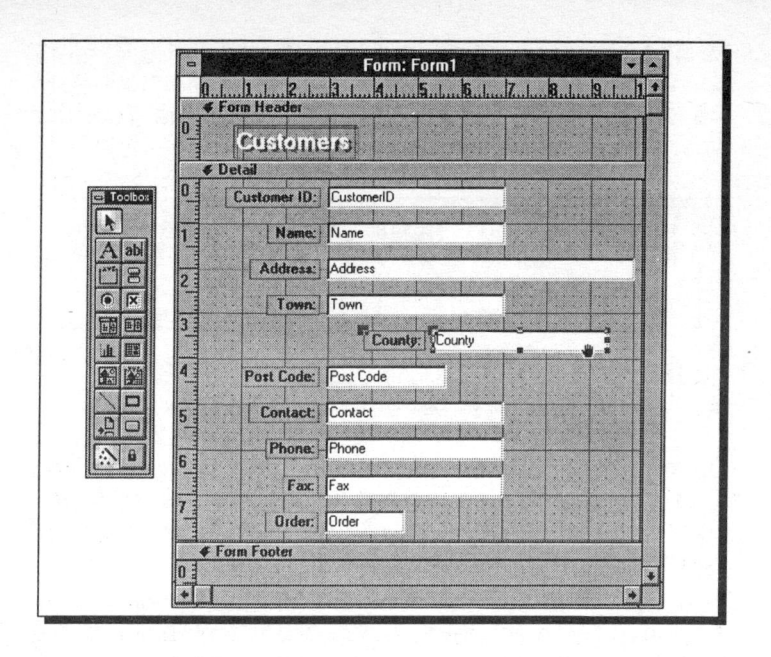

If you look more closely at the markers around the label and data boxes, you will see that they are of different size, as shown below.

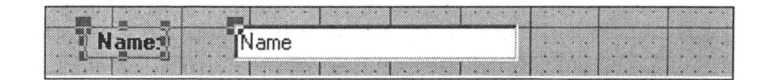

The larger ones are 'move' handles, while the smaller ones are 'size' handles. In the above example you can use the 'move' handles of either the label or the data box to move one independently of the other. The label box can also be sized. To size the data box, click on it so that the markers appear around it.

Boxes on a form can be made larger by simply pointing to the sizing handles and dragging them in the appropriate direction.

In addition to moving and enlarging label and data boxes, you can further customise a form with the use of the various new buttons that appear on the Tool bar when in Design View, shown below.

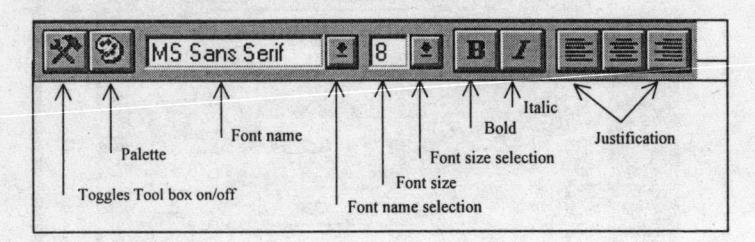

```
[Palette] [Toggles Tool box on/off] | MS Sans Serif [Font name / Font name selection] | 8 [Font size / Font size selection] | B [Bold] | I [Italic] | [Justification]
```

Do try and experiment with moving and sizing label and data boxes and also increasing their font size. If you don't like the result, simply don't save it. Skills gained here will be used in Report design.

You can find out the function of each tool on the Toolbox, by pointing to each icon and holding the mouse pointer on it. A description of its function will appear against the tool.

Using the Report Wizards

To produce a report of the Unpaid Invoices query, click the Report button on the Database window and select the Unpaid Invoices query in the New Report dialogue box. The steps for this procedure are identical to those used to produce a new form.

Next, click the **Report Wizards** button and select the Tabular report from the displayed 7 types of reports (the last one of these is the MS Word Mail Merge report, but to see it you must scroll down the list).

Now, select all the fields (except for the Paid? field) which are to appear on your report and click the **Next** button, then select the InvoiceID field as the sort field, and accept all subsequent default settings. The report is created for you and displayed.

However, this created report is not quite acceptable. The problem is mainly the fact that all text fields are left justified within their columns, while numerical fields are right justified. To change the position of the numeric fields, we must display the report in Design View. To do this, use the **View, Tool**b**ars** command, highlight the Report Design item in the **T**oolbars list of the displayed dialogue box and click the **S**how button, followed by the **Close** button.

This displays an additional Tool bar which allows you access to the Design View button. Clicking this button displays the Report as follows:

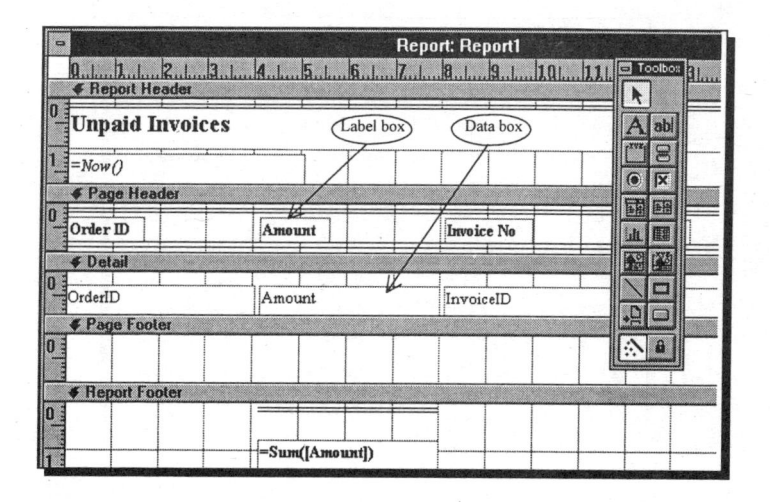

Use the mouse to move the Amount data box, the =Sum([Amount]) data box and the double lines above it to the left, and then right justify the text in the Amount label and data boxes and the formula at the bottom of the screen, as shown overleaf.

Unpaid Invoices

Order ID	Amount	Invoice No	Name
95002STO	£120.84	AD9501	VORTEX Co. Ltd
95006PAR	£103.52	AD9502	AVON Construction
95010WES	£99.32	AD9503	BARROWS Associates
95018GLO	£55.98	AD9504	STONEAGE Ltd
95025SIL	£180.22	AD9505	PARKWAY Gravel
95029WOI	£68.52	AD9506	WESTWOOD Ltd
95039EAL	£111.56	AD9507	GLOWORM Ltd
95045HIR	£123.45	AD9508	SILVERSMITH Co
95051EUR	£35.87	AD9509	WORMGLAZE Ltd
95064AVC	£58.95	AD9510	EALING Engines Design
	£958.23		

The corresponding report is now as follows:

This layout is obviously far more acceptable than that of the original report created by the Report Wizards.

* * *

Access has many more features than the ones covered in the limited space allocated to it here. However, we hope we have covered enough features of the program to have given you the confidence needed to make you want to explore Access more fully.

INDEX

A

Absolute address 101
Access database 137
Accessing menus 13
Active
   printer 51
   window 11
Adding
   fields to a query 162
   Office components 6
   printer 49
   records to a table ... 147
Aligning paragraphs 56
Application icons 7
AutoContent Wizard 127
AutoFormat 93
AutoSum icon 89
Axis labels (Excel) 115

B

Bullet insert 62

C

Changing
   active window 11
   axis labels (Excel) ... 115
   default options ... 32, 35
   fonts (Excel) 82
   fonts (Word) 54
   page layout 34
   paragraph style 29
   text (Word) 54
   text alignment (Excel) 82
   title in charts (Excel) 115
   view 30
Character font 54
Charts (Excel) 103

Chart types 116
ChartWizard 105
ClipArt 133
Close
   document 38
   window 13
Column chart 103
Context sensitive help ... 26
Control
   menu box (Word) 20
Copy command 39, 42
Copying sheets 98
Creating
   database query 161
   paragraph style 65
Criteria (Access) 163
Cue cards
   Access 138
   PowerPoint 126
Customising a chart 113
Cut command 39

D

Database
   criteria 163
   elements 140
   forms 146
   management 135
   query 157
   sorting 144
   tables 135, 141, 155
Default options 32
Delete text 43
Deleting fields & records 148
Design view (Access) .. 142
Dialogue boxes 11, 15
Display modes 30

Document
- basics 27
- edit 39
- formatting 53
- print preview 52
- printing 49
- screen displays 30
- styles 64
- templates 67
- views 30

Double line spacing 57
Drag & Drop text 43
Draw tool (PowerPoint) . 122

E
Edit
- copy, cut, paste 42
- function key (Excel) .. 79
- line (Excel) 75
- undo (Excel) 90
- undo (Word) 44,53

Editing
- documents 39
- relationships (Access) 154

Entering
- formulae & numbers . 87
- text (Excel) 87
- text (Word) 27

Excel
- examples & demos .. 72
- screen 70

F
Field (Access) 135
File
- close 10, 38
- command 14
- open, print 49
- run 3
- save 30
- summary info 37

Filling in
- a range by example .. 86
- a worksheet 79

Find & Replace 44
Finding records 147
Footers (Excel) 92, 94
Forms (Access) ... 146, 167
Formatting
- bar (Word) 20, 22, 23
- entries (Excel) 86
- page tabs 63
- quick keys 55
- styles (Excel) 83
- styles (Word) 64
- text 53

Freezing panes (Excel) . 102

G
Getting familiar with
- Excel 72
- PowerPoint 125
- Word 18

Go To
- box (word) 24

Grouping worksheets 77

H
Hanging indents 60
Hardware requirements .. 2
Headers (Excel) 92, 94
Help
- command 25
- menu (Access) 139
- menu (Excel) 73
- menu (PowerPoint) . 126
- menu (Word) 26

I
Icons MS-Office 7
Indentation 58

Insert
    bullets (Word) 62
    chart (Excel) 105
    ClipArt image 133
    worksheets 76
Inserting fields (Access) 148
Installing
    MS-Office 3
    Office components 6

L
Landscape orientation 33, 51
Layout
    mode 31
    page 34
Linking sheets 100
LPT1 port 49

M
Manipulating
    ranges 97
    windows 10
Margins 32
Master document 31
Maximise window 12
Menu bar (Word) . 13, 20, 21
Minimise window 12
Modify
    margins 32
    page layout 34
Mouse pointers 8
Moving
    around a document .. 28
    around a worksheet .. 74
    between sheets (Excel) 76
    blocks of text 43
    fields (Access) 148
    windows 11
MS-Office
    components 6
    icons 7

Multiple column charts . 113

N
Naming charts (Excel) .. 111
Normal
    mode 30
    style, template 29
Notes pages view 124

O
OLE 1
Opening a worksheet ... 85
Orientation 33, 51
Outline
    mode (Word) 30
    view (PowerPoint) .. 123

P
Page
    breaks 47
    set-up (Excel) 92
    set-up (Word) 32
    layout 34
    layout mode 31
    margins 32
    orientation 33, 51
    set-up 32
    tabs 63
Pane freeze 102
Paper settings 33
Paragraph
    alignment 56
    spacing 57
    style (Word) 65
Parallel printer port 49
Paste command 39, 42
Pick a look Wizard 131
Pie chart 116
Portrait orientation .. 33, 51

PowerPoint
   screen 120
   views 123
   Wizards 121
Pre-defined charts 111
Preview document 52
Print
   document 49
   orientation 33, 51
   preview 52, 92
   table view 149
   worksheet area .. 91, 95
Printer ports 49
Program icons 7
Pull down menus 14

Q
Query (Access) 157
Quick key formatting 55
Quick preview
   Excel 72
   Word 18

R
Record (Access) 135
Relational database 150
Relationships (Access) . 152
Relative address 101
Reports (Access) . 167, 170
Resizing windows 12
Restore
   buttons 20, 21
   windows 12
Replacing text 44
Ruler area (Word) ... 20, 22

S
Save As command .. 36, 87
Save
   icon 61, 107
   command 36, 84

Saving
   database designs ... 143
   charts (Excel) 111
Screen display
   Access 138
   Excel 70
   PowerPoint 120
   Word 19
Scroll bars 20, 22
Search & replace 44
Searching for records .. 147
Selecting
   range of cells 80
   style 64
   text 40
Selection
   bar (Word) 20, 22
   indicator (Excel) 75
Setting a print area 95
Shortcut
   keys, menus (Word) . 14
   menus (Excel) 77
Size windows 11
Slide
   sort view 124
   show view 125
Software requirements ... 2
Sorting database table . 144
Special characters 46
Spacing paragraphs 57
Spell Checker 48
Split box (Word) 20, 22
Spreadsheet charts 103
Starting
   Access 137
   Excel 69
   PowerPoint 119
   Word 17
Status bar 20, 24

Style
  formatting 64
  paragraph 65

T
Tab types 63
Table
  Access ... 135, 141, 155
  relationships 153
  Wizard 141
Templates (Word) ... 29, 67
Text
  alignment (Excel) 82
  copying 42
  deleting 43
  Drag & Drop 43
  editing 39
  enhancement 56
  finding & replacing ... 44
  formatting 53
  indentation 58
  moving 43
  selecting 40
  searching 44
Title
  bar 20, 21
  chart (Excel) 115
Toolbar (Word) 20, 21
Tools command 48

U
Undo
  command 44
  entry (Excel) 80
  formatting 53
Units of measurement ... 58
Using
  AutoSum icon 89
  database forms 146, 167
  Form Wizards 167
  functions (Excel) 88

Help (Access) 139
Help (Excel) 73
Help (PowerPoint) ... 126
Help (Word) 25
Report Wizards 170

V
View modes 30
Viewing
  table relationships .. 154
  workbook sheets 78
Views
  buttons 20, 23
  PowerPoint 123

W
Wildcard characters 166
Window command
  Excel 78
  Word 10
Wizards
  Access 141, 167
  Excel 105
  PowerPoint 121
Word
  examples & demos .. 12
  screen 19
  wrap 27
Workbook (Excel) 98
Worksheet
  grouping 77
  navigation 74
  opening 85
  order 77
  printing 91
WYSIWYG 31

Z
Zoom 26, 32

NOTES

COMPANION DISC TO THIS BOOK

This book contains many pages of file/program listings. There is no reason why you should spend hours typing them into your computer, unless you wish to do so, or need the practice.

The COMPANION DISC for this book comes in 3.5-inch format with all the example listings.

COMPANION DISCS for most books written by the same author(s) and published by BERNARD BABANI (publishing) LTD, are also available and are listed at the front of this book. Make sure you fill in your name and address and specify the book number and title in your order.

ORDERING INSTRUCTIONS

To obtain your copy of the companion disc, fill in the order form below or a copy of it, enclose a cheque (payable to **P.R.M. Oliver**) or a postal order, and send it to the address below.

Book No.	Book Name	Unit Price	Total Price
BP		£3.50	
BP		£3.50	
BP		£3.50	
Name .... Address		Sub-total	£.............
		P & P (@ 45p/disc)	£.............
		Total Due	£.............
Send to: P.R.M. Oliver, CSM, Pool, Redruth, Cornwall, TR15 3SE			

PLEASE NOTE

The author(s) are fully responsible for providing this Companion Disc service. The publishers of this book accept no responsibility for the supply, quality, or magnetic contents of the disc, or in respect of any damage, or injury that might be suffered or caused by its use.